Come Home to the Heart of God

Building Life on the 7 Pillars of God's Kingdom Family

Tom Elliff

ISBN 0-6330-9663-6

This book is a resource in two categories of the Christian Growth Study Plan. LS-
0034 in Family Ministry Leadership and LS-0068 in Leadership Development of the
Association Leader

Dewey Decimal Classification: 248.84
Subject Headings: FAMILY LIFE\CHRISTIAN LIFE

Unless otherwise indicated, all Scripture quotations are from the *Holman
Christian Standard Bible®,* copyright © 1999, 2000, 2001, 2002, 2003
by Holman Bible Publishers. Used by permission.
Scripture quotations marked NKJV are from the *New King James Version.*
Copyright © 1979, 1980, 1982, Thomas Nelson, Inc., Publishers.
Scripture quotations marked KJV are from the *King James Version.*

To order additional copies of this resource: WRITE LifeWay Church Resources
Customer Service; One LifeWay Plaza; Nashville, TN 37234-0113;
FAX order to (615) 251-5933; PHONE (800) 458-2772;
E-MAIL to *customerservice@lifeway.com;* ORDER ONLINE at *www.lifeway.com;*
or VISIT the LifeWay Christian Store serving you.

Printed in the United States of America

Leadership and Adult Publishing
LifeWay Church Resources
One LifeWay Plaza
Nashville, TN 37234-0175

Contents

About the Author

A former president of the Southern Baptist Convention and the SBC Pastor's Conference, Tom Elliff has led crusades and conferences across the United States and in many foreign countries. He is a graduate of Ouchita Baptist University and Southwestern Baptist Theological Seminary, serving earlier pastorates in Arkansas, Texas, Oklahoma, and Colorado. For two years, the Elliffs were commissioned by the Foreign Mission Board (now the International Mission Board) of the Southern Baptist Convention, and ministered in Zimbabwe, Africa. In addition to their church's radio and television ministry, the Elliffs often have been guests on nationwide broadcasts addressing family issues. Tom chaired the Southern Baptist Council on Family Life.

Tom has been a contributing author to several publications, including *MasterLife*, the *Family Worship Bible*, and *The Disciple's Study Bible*. He is the author of several books by Broadman & Holman, including *Unbreakable! The Seven Pillars of a Kingdom Family, Letters to Lovers, Praying for Others,* and *The Pathway to God's Presence*. He also has authored *A Passion for Prayer,* published by Crossway. Along with Robert G. Witty, he co-authored *In Their Own Words* (Broadman & Holman).

A third generation Baptist pastor, Tom and his wife Jeannie, reside in Oklahoma City, Oklahoma, where for more than 18 years he has pastored the First Southern Baptist Church in Del City. they are the parents of four children and grandparents of 18 grandchildren. Each of their children, and their children's families, is active in church ministry and missions.

Introduction

Come Home to the Heart of God is more than the title of this study. It is an exciting movement to restore the family to God's intended purpose. The end result is a life—and a family—that honors God, lives out His principles, effectively carries the gospel to the nations, and passes along a legacy of faith to succeeding generations.

Whether you are single or married, young or old, this workbook is for you. In it you will find practical help as a member of God's Kingdom Family. You are becoming part of a movement that will change your life, strengthen your home, revolutionize your church and community, and reach the nations for Christ.

Come Home to the Heart of God is written in an interactive format to enhance your learning and application of the truths found in Scripture. Unless otherwise noted, all Scriptures are from the *Holman Christian Standard Version* of the Bible. Although this is the preferred translation, most translations will be suitable to use.

I encourage you to complete each activity. Unless asked to do so, don't answer the questions as you know they *should* be answered, as you *once* would have answered them, or as you would *like* to answer them. Be honest about where you are *now* in your journey.

If possible, each week you should attend a small-group session. During this hour-long session, you will discuss the content you studied the previous week, share insights, encourage one another, and pray together. Working through this material with at least one accountability partner will greatly enhance the value of this study.

Welcome to the journey!

Yours for Kingdom Families,
Tom Elliff

WEEK ONE

Your Foundation:
The Unseen Essential

"Which of you, wanting to build a tower, doesn't first sit down and calculate the cost, to see if he has enough to complete it?" (Luke 14:28)

The summer heat, beat back by the straining air conditioner, was still no match for the temperature of the discussion in the living room. I had visited in this home before, but never under these circumstances. A seemingly stable, faithful family was falling apart.

I don't remember everything I said in an attempt to buy time for a miracle. But I do remember standing on the front porch as I was preparing to leave. I was trying my best to convey some sense of hope. In a lame attempt to change subjects, the husband pointed to a crack in the brick veneer, a crack I traced, first up the roofline, then all the way to the foundation, which had also cracked and settled. The foundation of this house was falling apart.

Day One
How Firm Is Your Foundation?

"Everyone who hears these words of Mine and acts on them will be like a sensible man who built his house on the rock" (Matt. 7:24).

The house this family lived in was the least of their worries. Their *home* was in a far more serious condition. The pressures of life were revealing that this family, like the house in which they lived, was built on something other than a solid foundation.

Nothing is more critical to a building than its foundation. Everything rests on it. Beautiful buildings have been abandoned because they rested on poor foundations.

One of the parables in the Bible talks about the importance of a firm foundation. Read this story from Matthew 7:24-27.

"Everyone who hears these words of Mine and acts on them will be like a sensible man who built his house on the rock. The rain fell, the rivers rose, and the winds blew and pounded that house. Yet it didn't collapse, because its foundation was on the rock. But everyone who hears these words of Mine and doesn't act on them will be like a foolish man who built his house on the sand. The rain fell, the rivers rose, the winds blew and pounded that house, and it collapsed. And its collapse was great!"

Notice that the circumstances were the same: *"The rain fell, the rivers rose, and the winds blew and pounded that house."* But because the foundations were different, the results were different.

What storm have you experienced recently? _____

_____

Where did you turn when the storm came your way?
❑ prayer and the Bible   ❑ other people
❑ a compulsive habit such as eating, drug use, etc.

> **Nothing is more critical to a building than its foundation.**

❏ seclusion, distancing yourself from others
❏ other _____

What feelings did you have during the worst part of the storm?
❏ anger   ❏ doubt
❏ fear   ❏ calmness
❏ peace   ❏ other _____

How did you feel after the storm had passed?
❏ relief   ❏ sense of doom
❏ peace   ❏ anger
❏ stronger than before   ❏ other _____

Job questioned his very existence.

The Old Testament man Job questioned his very existence when his life turned from comfortable to crumbled. He lost his children, his house, his livestock, and his health but not his faith in God. His wife encouraged him to *"Curse God and die!"* (Job 2:9, NKJV). Fill in the blanks of Job's response, found in Job 2:10:

"Shall we indeed accept _____ from God, and shall we not accept _____?"

Even Job's friends—Eliphaz, Bildad, and Zophar—were only helpful for a while. Chapter two tells us that they *"sat down with him on the ground seven days and seven nights, and no one spoke a word to him, for they saw that his grief was very great"* (v. 13, NKJV).

Has someone come alongside you when you were suffering? Write the name (or initials) of this person in the margin.

Check any of the following that reflect advice you've received.
❏ "Curse God and die!"
❏ "Have faith in God. He will never fail you."
❏ "This must be because of sin in your life. Confess your sin. Get right with God."
❏ "Just get over it."
❏ "Oh, yeah, that's nothing, I experienced…."
❏ "I will stand beside you and help in any way I can."

God was silent for a long time while Job suffered. The discourse between Job and his friends filled 35 chapters. Finally, God broke His silence with a series of questions and statements to Job. We read in chapter 38, verse 4: *"Where were you when I laid the foundations of the earth? Tell Me, if you have understanding"* (NKJV).

Humbled, Job replied, *"I am vile; what shall I answer You? I lay my hand over my mouth"* (40:4, NKJV).

How would you reply to God's discourse?
❑ "Don't bother me. I'm suffering."
❑ "I'll weigh Your advice against that of my friends."
❑ "I want to respond like Job, in humility to my Creator."

God didn't address Job's suffering or tell him He would provide divine justice. He was letting Job see that because He had laid the earth's very foundation, He was in control.

From the beginning of Job's story, God reminds us this man *"was blameless and upright, and one who feared God and shunned evil"* (1:1, NKJV). At the end of the story, Job's character is strengthened, not shaken. God still refers to Job as His servant. Job's family and fortune were important to him, but not nearly as important as his faith in God.

Do you know anyone who has this kind of faith? Write that person's name in the margin.

What do you see in this person's faith that makes it so exemplary?

_____

_____

Is this kind of faith unique only to him or her? ❑ yes   ❑ no

How willing are you to listen to God's Word and act upon what He says?

God didn't address Job's suffering.

Day Two
On What Foundation Are You Building?

"No one can lay any other foundation than what has been laid—that is, Jesus Christ" (1 Cor. 3:11).

This book is about the family, but it starts with you.

This book is about the family, but it starts with you. You may be a family of one, or your family might include a spouse, children, parents, grandparents, or any combination of these.

Throughout this workbook you will see references to God's Kingdom Family. This term is used to describe a clearly defined biblical concept. The two most commonly-used analogies that describe God's unique relationship with His people are *kingdom* and *family*.

Look up the following verses and mark whether they refer to *kingdom* ("K") or *family* ("F"). As you read them, note the benefits of being a citizen of God's Kingdom and a member of His family.

___ Romans 8:15-17 _____

___ Galatians 4:6-7 _____

___ Ephesians 2:19-20 _____

___ Philippians 3:20 _____

___ 1 John 3:1-2 _____

According to these verses, what is the best part of being a citizen of God's Kingdom?

_____

What is the best part of being a member of God's family?

_____

If you have by faith repented of your sin and believed in Christ and His redeeming work on the cross, you possess the eternal life of your resurrected Savior. You have been born again into His family!

Who else in your circle of acquaintances is a member of God's Kingdom Family? This list might include people in your family, church, school, neighborhood, or workplace. Write their names in the margin.

On what basis do you consider these people to be genuine members of God's Kingdom Family? (See John 14:6.)

Every genuine member of God's Kingdom Family wants others to be part of the family as well. The purpose of this workbook is to show you how you can build God's Kingdom principles into your own earthly family. Then, together, you can share the love of Christ with those around you and around the world.

Whom do you include in your personal family? Write their names in the margin.

Early in my experience as a pastor, I found myself in an increasing number of troubling family situations for which I had no genuinely effective solution. The fact that people were willing to come to a relatively inexperienced minister with their problems was more an indication of their desperation than my abilities! For a few years I did my best in giving as much advice as I could. Most of my counsel was simply homespun wisdom with a little Scripture thrown. Soon I noticed that the same people were returning again and again. In other words, nothing was really happening to produce change in their lives or in their homes.

I remember lamenting this problem with an older pastor and personal mentor. "You know, Tom," he commented thoughtfully, "I've discovered that most people's problems are not solved when they come to me but when they come to Christ. For that reason I

You will learn how to build God's Kingdom principles into your family.

never proceed with any kind of counseling—personal or family—until I am certain of an individual's relationship with Christ. My responsibility is showing them how to find the answers for their problems in God's Word. But if they don't know Him and if they don't respect His Word, I'm just wasting my time and theirs."

Take your spiritual temperature.

This next activity is of eternal importance. Below you see a hollow tube that resembles a thermometer. Use this diagram to plot your spiritual temperature. You'll not see a mark to designate what "normal" is. In this case, it's better to be hot than cold. Check any of the conditions that apply to your life. Add more items as necessary to describe the condition of your spiritual life.

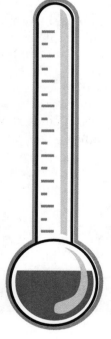

My life is radically different because I know Christ.

I know Christ, but I live in disobedience to Him in some areas of my life.

By faith, I repented of sin and believed in Christ alone as Savior.

God provides the only foundation on which to build my life.

God loves me unconditionally and will forgive me of my sin if I confess those sins.

I realize that I will go into eternity without God if I died tonight.

Come Home to the Heart of God is about building God's Kingdom Family, but it is also about choices. One choice is paramount: the choice to turn from your way and to trust in Christ alone as your personal Savior. To build a Kingdom Family you must first be a member of God's own kingdom family. You must know Christ personally and walk with Him in a daily relationship.

Are you confident that you have genuinely experienced God's love and forgiveness in Christ? ❑ yes   ❑ no

If not, commit your life to Him now. Settle this issue now. Read John 1:12, and express your faith in a prayer like the one below: *Jesus, I confess that I am a sinner, living in my own way. I thank you for loving me and dying on the cross as payment for my sin. I know that you were raised from the dead and are alive today. Right now, I want to receive you by faith, trusting in You as my Lord and Savior. Thank You for saving me and for Your gift of eternal life. Amen.*

If you've prayed this prayer, write today's date in the margin.

Perhaps you have been walking with the Lord for some time and you know how essential that relationship is to building a strong foundation in your life. Are you where you want to be in your personal relationship with Jesus?

How is your relationship with Jesus?

Write a prayer affirming your relationship with Jesus and expressing your desire to build your life on Him.

_____

_____

Day Three
Put Your Story in Writing

"I have written these things to you who believe in the name of the Son of God, so that you may know that you have eternal life" (1 John 5:13).

At our church we have a *Book of Life* containing the written testimonies of our members. We often read these records of individual conversion experiences on special occasions like anniversaries or funerals. Sometimes this is the first time family members and friends hear the details of how this person came to know Christ. Today you have the privilege of doing what our members do.

When we first developed our *Book of Life,* one of our church members shared about it with her ailing mother. "I want to do that!" said her mother, who then shared her testimony as her daughter recorded it. A week later, at her funeral, I had the privilege of reading that testimony with those who were present.

This woman left her family a legacy of faith.

This precious saint left a legacy for her children and grandchildren. Obviously, they were not present when she had trusted Christ. But by writing down the details, she was able to pass along the importance of her faith. How comforting for her family and friends to know without a doubt that she was in the presence of the Savior in Whom she had put her faith.

Do you know a person like the woman above? If so, write the name of this person and their relation to you in the margin.

In his second letter to Timothy, the apostle Paul reminds his young disciple that the sincere faith Timothy possessed was first in his grandmother, Lois, and his mother, Eunice (2 Tim. 1:5). They had passed on to him a legacy of faith.

Has anyone in your family passed on their legacy of faith to you? If so, write their name in the margin.

Timothy's grandmother made certain that the torch of her faith was passed to her daughter who then passed it to her own son. On more than one occasion I have talked with parents whose children have "strayed from the faith." Admittedly, we cannot discount the power of personal choice. But neither can we pass the buck when it comes to our responsibility for nurturing a growing sense of spiritual heritage in our own family.

Do you have family and friends who do not know of your faith in Christ? ❏ yes   ❏ no

Now it's time to write *your* testimony of faith! If you've never written down the story of how you came to Christ, this activity will give you a chance to do so. Don't be overwhelmed. Don't write words to impress anyone; be yourself. Fill in the blanks that follow. In your small group this week, you will have an opportunity to share your story with others.

It's time to write *your* testimony of faith.

I, _____, have the confidence that if I were to die today, I would spend my forever in heaven.

If I were to die today and stand before God, and He were to say to me, "Why should I let you into My heaven?," I would respond:

_____

_____

_____

As best I recall, this took place at _____
when I was _____ years of age. When I think about that important event, I remember:

_____

_____

_____

_____

Since I received Christ, I can see God's hand at work changing me and equipping me for His service in the following ways:

_____

_____

I was scripturally baptized at: _____

Approximate date: _____

Some of the people whom the Lord used to bring me to Christ:

_____

_____

Your signature

_____

Your friend, teacher, or group facilitator

_____

Your pastor

You've done important work.

Congratulations! You have taken steps to leave a legacy of faith for your family. As an end to this day's hard work, meditate on today's verse (1 John 5:13). How will others know they have eternal life because of the story you've shared?

_____

_____

Day Four
Build a Strong Foundation, Part One

"Wisdom has built her house; she has carved out her seven pillars" (Prov. 9:1).

The outline from which this workbook is developed is based on the Kingdom Family Commitment which you can read in its entirety on page 24. You will read through an overview of this commitment during the next two days. Tomorrow you will have an opportunity to sign this commitment.

The Preamble of the commitment reads as follows:

I am a member of God's Kingdom Family. I have by faith repented of my sin, believed on Christ as my Lord and Savior, and received His gift of forgiveness and eternal life. By the miracle of God's grace, I am both a citizen of His kingdom and a member of His family. His subject and His child, His bond slave and a joint heir with Him, His battle-ready soldier and His bride. It is now my desire to glorify the Lord by giving my own earthly family relationships and the interest and care they so richly deserve. With the balance of my life and relying on the leadership of God's Spirit, I will commit to God's plan for my life and family by:

Honoring God's Authority
Respecting Human Life
Exercising Moral Purity
Serving My Church
Using Time Wisely
Practicing Biblical Stewardship
Sharing the Gospel of Jesus Christ

To encourage you in your study, here is a brief summary of each pillar and the biblical basis for each. As you read each pillar, ask yourself several questions listed after the overview.

Pillar One: Honoring God's Authority

God, as Sovereign Creator and Sustainer of all, holds Ultimate Authority over His creation. By establishing the family, God has provided a unique setting in which each individual should come to understand and respect authority. I will glorify God by surrendering every area of my life to Him and by offering godly respect in all my earthly relationships, starting in my family.

The biblical basis for this pillar includes some of the following Scriptures. Read these and write any significance they have regarding the area of authority.

Romans 12:1-2 _____

Romans 13:1-7 _____

1 Corinthians 10:31 _____

Ephesians 5:21 _____

Ephesians 6:1-4 _____

What difference does it make in a person's life if God is the Ultimate Authority?

_____

What areas might be difficult to surrender as a person places God in the position of Ultimate Authority?

_____

Pillar Two: Respecting Human Life

Pillar Two: Respecting Human Life

Human life is a gift from God and is of transcendent worth. It is to be treasured, protected, encouraged, and loved from the moment of conception until the moment of death. I know that each member of my family must ultimately give an account to God, and forgiveness of sin and eternal life in heaven require personal repentance of sin and faith in Christ. I will honor God by expressing self-sacrificial love to each of my family members throughout the entirety of their lives.

The biblical basis for pillar two includes some of the following Scriptures. Read these and write any significance they have regarding respect for human life.

Exodus 20:13 _____

Psalm 139:13-18 _____

Proverbs 16:31 _____

What behaviors, decisions, and attitudes show that a person has respect for human life? Write your answer in the margin.

18

What obstacles might interfere with respecting life?

_____

Pillar Three: Exercising Moral Purity

God has established the family as His first institution on earth. It is worthy of my most noble aspirations and commitments, including my commitment to moral purity, marital fidelity, and Christ-like love for each family member. Because marriage is a picture of Christ's faithfulness to His bride, the church, and because the family is a picture of the Father's faithfulness to His children, I will honor the Lord by being faithful and pure.

The biblical basis for this pillar includes some of the following Scriptures. Read these and write a decision that each verse or passage compels you to make.

Exodus 20:14 _____

Job 31:1 _____

Matthew 5:27-30 _____

1 Corinthians 6:18-20 _____

What behaviors are involved if a person were committed to be morally pure?

_____

What roadblocks lie ahead of a person trying to show Christlike love to each family member regardless of their age or stage of life?

_____

Thank God for being faithful as you are obedient in studying His Word and committing to these pillars of a strong foundation.

Day Five
Build a Strong Foundation, Part Two

"The whole building is being fitted together in Him and is growing into a holy sanctuary in the Lord, in whom you also are being built together for God's dwelling in the Spirit" (Eph. 2:21-22).

Today you will finish your overview of the seven pillars. You also have an opportunity to sign a commitment embracing these pillars as the key to strengthening your life and family.

Pillar Four: Serving My Church

Pillar Four: Serving My Church
The church is the bride of Christ, comprised of all the redeemed whom God will, one day, take to heaven. By exalting Christ, resting on the sufficiency of His Word, and giving place to the ministry of the Spirit, the local church becomes the means by which spiritual growth is promoted and the ministry of Christ is brought to my family, my community, and to the world. I will support and encourage my family to support our local church with faithful attendance, diligent service, generous and God-honoring giving, and loving cooperation.

The biblical basis for pillar four includes some of the following Scriptures. Read these and write how each impacts your service in your church.

Matthew 16:16-18 _____

Ephesians 4:11-16 _____

Ephesians 5:25-26 _____

Hebrews 10:24-25 _____

Why should the local church be an avenue of spiritual growth and ministry in a person's life?

_____

Name the ways you are effectively serving God now through your service in your church.

Pillar Five: Using Time Wisely

Time is a resource given to each person by God. My use of it, especially in matters related to my family, reflects my esteem for God. One day I will give an account to Him for how I have spent the time He entrusted to me. As I order my life in concert with His will, I will have sufficient time for personal growth through prayer, for the study of God's Word, and for fulfilling every God-given responsibility related to my family.

The biblical basis for this pillar includes some of the following Scriptures. Read these and write any significance they have in following God's will, especially as it applies to time.

Deuteronomy 6:6-7 _____

Psalm 90:12 _____

Luke 12:16-21 _____

Ephesians 5:15-16 _____

2 Timothy 3:15 _____

List in the margin some of the God-given responsibilities in a family.

Everyone has the same amount of time in a day. However, it seems that some people have more time to get important things done. What challenges lie ahead of you as you begin to prioritize your time? Write these in the margin.

Pillar Six: Practicing Biblical Stewardship

God has provided material resources so that I may glorify Him through the exercise of faithful stewardship over them. I will be held accountable for this stewardship. Therefore, I will diligently seek my

Pillar Six: Practicing Biblical Stewardship

Master's best interests in the way I earn money, expend it for life's needs, use it to touch the lives of others, and give it for the support of His work through my local church.

The biblical basis for pillar six includes some of the following Scriptures. Read these and write any significance they have regarding stewardship.

Genesis 1:28 _____

Proverbs 3:9-10 _____

Malachi 3:8-11 _____

Luke 6:38 _____

1 Corinthians 16:1-2 _____

2 Corinthians 9:7-8 _____

Do you *really* believe everything you have belongs to God?
❑ yes   ❑ no

How is this belief currently affecting the way you are managing your resources?

_____

_____

_____

Pillar Seven: Sharing the Gospel of Jesus Christ

Pillar Seven: Sharing the Gospel of Jesus Christ
The greatest and most noble purpose in life is to glorify the Lord through the fulfillment of His Great Commission. I will glorify the Lord by sharing my faith with my family and by joining with them and others in specific activities that cultivate a passion for fulfilling the Great Commission.

The biblical basis for this pillar includes some of the following Scriptures. After reading each Scripture, write what you are doing now to comply with it.

Matthew 28:19-20 _____

John 4:37-42 _____

Acts 1:8 _____

Romans 1:16 _____

Revelation 22:17 _____

What roadblocks get in the way of sharing the gospel with others?

_____

_____

Perhaps you've heard that sharing the gospel is more difficult to do with family members. Why is this so? Or have you experienced the opposite?

_____

_____

These are the seven pillars of God's Kingdom Family. Will you determine to build your life on these pillars? Are you willing to share that determination with your spouse (if you are married) and with others close to you? Will you allow these people to hold you accountable for your commitment? If so, turn the page and sign the Kingdom Family Commitment.

Will you build your life on these pillars?

23

Kingdom Family Commitment

I am a member of God's Kingdom Family. I have by faith repented of my sin, believed on Christ as my Lord and Savior, and received His gift of forgiveness and eternal life. By the miracle of God's grace, I am both a citizen of His kingdom and a member of His family. His subject and His child, His bond slave and a joint heir with Him, His battle-ready soldier and His bride. It is now my desire to glorify the Lord by giving my own earthly family relationships and the interest and care they so richly deserve. With the balance of my life and relying on the leadership of God's Spirit, I will commit to God's plan for my life and family by:

Honoring God's Authority
Respecting Human Life
Exercising Moral Purity
Serving My Church
Using Time Wisely
Practicing Biblical Stewardship
Sharing the Gospel of Jesus Christ

I commit to this study of *Come Home to the Heart of God*. By God's grace, my life and family will be founded on Christ and strengthened by the seven pillars of God's Kingdom Family.

_____   _____
Signed   Date

_____   _____
Accountability partner, teacher,   Date
or facilitator

WEEK TWO

Honoring God's Authority

"Brothers, by the mercies of God, I urge you to present your bodies as a living sacrifice, holy and pleasing to God; this is your spiritual worship. Do not be conformed to this age, but be transformed by the renewing of your mind, so that you may discern what is the good, pleasing, and perfect will of God" (Rom. 12:1-2).

It was a cold night in early spring, and I was a college student serving as a summer missionary. For that week, I was a camp counselor in northern Maine. Before I opened the door to the bunkhouse, I could hear the bedlam taking place inside. It was a free-for-all, and I was about to bring it to an end.

"Lights out!" I shouted. "Everyone get in his own bunk! Nobody gets up or goes out! And nobody is to say another word." For a moment I believe we were all surprised by the immediacy of the response. It became perfectly quiet, but only for a moment. Out of the darkness came the recognizable voice of one of my problem kids: "Are you asking us or telling us?"

"I'm telling you!" I blasted back in return.

"That's all I wanted to know," he said, rolling over and soon going to sleep.

In his question was rooted the basic issue of authority.

Day 1
No Other Gods

"I am the LORD your God, who brought you out of the land of Egypt, out of the place of slavery. Do not have other gods besides Me" (Ex. 20:2-3).

Honoring God's authority is the first of the seven pillars necessary for building God's Kingdom Family. Last week you read an overview of this pillar and some of the Scriptures that support this principle. Now you will dig deeper in your study of God's authority.

God delivered the Israelites.

Let's go back a few thousand years. God delivered the Hebrew people from years of bondage in Egypt. They saw the waves of the Red Sea crash behind them as they walked across dry land to freedom. Exodus 14:31 says that *"when Israel saw the great power that the LORD used against the Egyptians, the people feared the LORD and believed in Him and in His servant Moses."* God delivered them!

Name a difficult situation from which you have been delivered.

_____

How did God get you through that situation?
❏ He provided strength to persevere.
❏ He removed the problem.
❏ He deepened my relationship with Him.
❏ He sent people to encourage me.
❏ other _____

The Hebrew people were so joyful in being delivered that they broke out in song. You can find this song in Exodus chapter 15. List seven specific actions God took in delivering His people.

1. _____

2. _____

3. _____

4. _____

5. _____

6. _____

7. _____

The people praised the Lord specifically. Are you specific when you praise God? Take a few minutes now to thank God specifically for something He has done for you today.

The thousands of Israelites traveled through the desert and encountered many troubling situations. Yet, God was constantly there as He provided guidance, food, water, and strength over their enemies. In Exodus 13:21-22, we read that God provided specifically for the people. Fill in the blanks to finish the verses.

"The LORD went ahead of them _____ to lead them on their way during the day and _____ to give them light at night, so that they could travel day or night. The pillar of cloud by day and the pillar of fire by night never left its place in front of the people."

What are some ways God has guided you on your journey in life?
❏ His written Word has instructed me.
❏ I've learned about His forgiveness through mistakes I've made.
❏ I recognize God's voice in prayer.
❏ I've received wisdom through counsel from godly friends.

Human nature lets us forget God's mercy and grace if things don't go as we think they should. When the Israelites became hungry, they grumbled and cried out to Moses and Aaron: *"If only we had died by the LORD's hand in the land of Egypt"* (Ex. 16:3). Read a few verses further in this chapter to discover how God provided for their hunger. Fill in the blanks to know what God provided.

Are you specific when you praise God?

"The LORD spoke to Moses, 'I have heard the complaints of the Israelites. Tell them: At twilight you will eat _____, and in the morning you will eat _____ until you are full. Then you will know that I am the LORD your God' " (16:12).

And, God did as He promised. *"At evening quail came and covered the camp. In the morning there was a layer of dew all around the camp. When the layer of dew evaporated, there on the desert surface were fine flakes, as fine as frost on the ground"* (16:13-14).

While we might be quick to fault the Israelites for complaining, sometimes we complain and grumble when our needs are not met.

What areas of your life are you tempted to grumble about?
- ❏ not enough money to pay bills
- ❏ unanswered prayer
- ❏ difficult people
- ❏ persecution from non-believers
- ❏ no job
- ❏ health concerns
- ❏ unmet expectations
- ❏ other _____

What areas of your life are you tempted to grumble about?

These and other events happened in the early days of their pilgrimage toward the Promised Land. The Israelites had to rely completely on God to take care of them. Sometimes they were obedient; sometimes they were not. However, God was teaching them that He was reliable and worthy of their faith and trust.

Before he died, Moses explained that all God had done for Israel during their 40 years of wandering in the wilderness was for the purpose of teaching them a critical lesson on authority and faith. Read Deuteronomy 8:1-3. Write in the margin the major lesson that God wanted Israel to learn.

Because God was worthy, He gave His people rules to follow and commanded their obedience. When God delivered the Ten Commandments through Moses, He began with a reminder and a command: *"I am the LORD your God, who brought you out of the land of Egypt, out of the place of slavery. Do not have other gods besides Me"* (Ex. 20:2-3).

What does *"Do not have other gods besides Me"* mean? Check each statement that applies.

❑ I must love God and worship Him only.

❑ I must look to God's written Word, the Bible, for wisdom in making decisions.

❑ God must be the ultimate authority in my life.

Write in the margin additional thoughts you have about this phrase.

Apart from our understanding and acceptance of this command, the other commandments are scarcely worth our consideration. It is an all-or-nothing proposition. God must be the ultimate authority in our lives.

Are you rejecting God's authority by refusing to obey His principles in a specific area of your life? How do you think God must respond to your disobedience because of His love for you?

How will God respond to your dis- obedience?

_____

_____

Israel's history is important. Paul reminds us that *"whatever was written before was written for our instruction, so that through our endurance and through the encouragement of the Scriptures we may have hope"* (Rom. 15:4). Pause now to thank God for how He provided for the Israelites and how He will provide for you in the coming days.

Day 2
Who Is Your Authority?

"Hear, O Israel: The LORD our God, the LORD is one!" (Deut. 6:4)

One of the most disturbing trends in public education today is the attempt to remove any reference to God from the classroom.

Where this attempt is successful, an equal rise in disciplinary problems has occurred. After all, if a student's respect for others is not rooted in a reverence for God, then it is reserved for those who can exert the most power, overwhelm with humanistic reason, or strongly appeal to a person's naturally rebellious tendencies. Without God, students have only this response, "I will obey you to the extent you either impress or intimidate me."

Name a recent event that reflects the trend mentioned above.

_____

_____

Whom did this event affect?
❏ students   ❏ teachers
❏ administrators   ❏ community
❏ others _____

What was the effect? _____

_____

A proper understanding of God and a corresponding reverence for Him changes the outcome of a situation. With these in place, an authority figure is viewed both as a person—and thereby deserving the respect due to all people—and as a representative of God's appointed authority. Respect becomes a matter affecting an individual's relationship with God as well as classroom behavior.

Where should we learn to revere God?

Where should we learn this understanding and reverence for God? Is it the responsibility of the church? The school? The government? None of these institutions can function well without acknowledging God's sovereignty. God intends for the family, His first institution, to be the primary setting in which each of us is to develop a proper understanding and respect for Him and for the authority figures He places in our lives.

Check each person below who is an authority figure in your life.

	1 no problem	5 sometimes easy, sometimes difficult	10 it's a real challenge
❑ boss/supervisor			
❑ government			
❑ pastor			
❑ teacher			
❑ parent			
❑ spouse			
❑ other			

On a scale of 1-10, how easy—or difficult—is it to submit to their authority? Plot your answer on the line beside each.

The Kingdom Family Commitment begins, *God, as Sovereign Creator and Sustainer of all, holds Ultimate Authority over His creation.* This is an affirmation of the first commandment, *"Do not have other gods besides Me."* Settling this issue in your heart will help in several ways in your life.

First, it will simplify your relationship to authority. Imagine how unique and difficult it was for the nations in Moses' day to grasp the concept of one God. The existence of so many gods created enormous complications. Each was in charge of specific areas of life and had to be appealed to in the appropriate fashion.

Unfortunately, the problem of worshiping many gods wasn't resolved in Moses' time. The apostle Paul addressed a crowd in Athens with the same problem. Read about his encounter with the people in Acts 17:16-29.

Settling the issue of God as Ultimate Authority will help your life in many ways.

Paul acknowledged that the people were very religious. However, he remarks, with amazement, *"As I was passing through and observing the objects of your worship, I even found an altar on which was inscribed:* TO AN _____ GOD*"* (v. 23).

The people wanted to ensure that their bases were covered, so that they created an unknown god, one to cover anything they might have missed.

Does the God of Moses—the Almighty God—lack anything so that you would have to create another god? Read the verse in the margin and underline the words or phrases for your answer.

My God will supply all your needs according to His riches in glory in Christ Jesus (Phil. 4:19).

Back in Moses' time, altars to gods were everywhere, and sacrifices ran the gamut from hares to humans. Abraham arrived at Canaan, the crossroads of the world, with the message that only one God existed. He further complicated the issue by insisting that the way to God was by faith rather than works. That message kept him and his descendants in constant conflict with their neighbors, producing tensions that ultimately led to an extended period of slavery in Egypt. When God delivered the people under Moses' leadership, they set their faces toward the Promised Land. But on their journey homeward, God made it perfectly clear that He alone was to be in charge. This is the message Moses brought back from Mt. Sinai: *"Do not have other gods besides* [in addition to, or in front of] *Me."*

The first commandment, as with all of God's commandments, was to be established clearly and communicated through the *family*.

Read the passage below. Circle the action words that direct you to teach the next generation.
"Listen, Israel: The LORD *our God, the* LORD *is One. Love the* LORD *your God with all your heart, with all your soul, and with all your strength. These words that I am giving you today are to be in your heart. Repeat them to your children. Talk about them when you sit in your house and when you walk along the road, when you lie down and when you get up* (Deut. 6:4-7).

How do you *impress* the commandments on your children as you talk, sit, walk, lie down, and get up? If you don't have children of your own, how can you communicate this truth to those in your extended family or those you see at church or in your community?

_____

_____

Israel's prosperity in the land of promise was tied directly to the effectiveness with which these principles were embraced and taught to succeeding generations. God stated that compliance with them was essential *"so that you may prosper and multiply greatly"* (Deut. 6:3).

The phrase *may prosper and multiply greatly* refers back to the covenant God made with Abraham, found in Genesis 15:5. Abraham is known as *"the father of all who believe"* (Rom. 4:11). Abraham had only two sons by a physical birth, but, in a spiritual sense, he is the father of all of us who are believers.

What person, in addition to Abraham, would you recognize as your spiritual father or teacher? _____

Pause to offer a word of thanks to God for this person. Perhaps you might want to write this person a note of thanks for the influence he (or she) has had in your life.

Day 3
Submit to Every Authority
"Submit to every human institution because of the Lord" (1 Pet. 2:13).

Yesterday you listed several people to whom you are under authority. The apostle Paul talked about submitting to authority in Romans 13:1. Fill in the blanks in the verse on the next page.

God said to Abraham, "Look at the sky and count the stars, if you are able to count them. ... Your off-spring will be that numerous" (Gen. 15:5).

Everyone must _____ to the governing authorities, for there is _____ authority except from _____, and those that exist are instituted by _____.

In verse 4, Paul says that the government is "_____ servant."

Why should we submit to the authorities?

1.

2.

In verse 5, we read two reasons why we are to submit to the authorities. What are these reasons? Write them in the margin.

We are to submit to authorities not only because we could be punished if we disobey, but also because of *our conscience.* The author of Hebrews encourages us with the following: *We are convinced that we have a clear conscience, wanting to conduct ourselves honorably in everything* (13:18). This follows the verse that gives instruction to obey leaders and submit to their authority.

Fill in the blanks of Hebrews 13:17:
Obey your _____ and _____ to them, for they keep watch over your souls as those who give an account, so that they can do this with _____ and not with _____.

In recent years, we have heard numerous stories of leaders who disobeyed the rules. Some have been caught and have been punished. Others seem to get off easy.

Respond to the following statements with T (True) or F (False).
_____ God expects me only to follow those leaders who revere Him.
_____ Unless commanded to renounce or disobey God, I should submit to all authority, whether or not they follow God.

Although challenging, we are commanded to submit to our authorities whether or not they follow God. If we do not submit to them, it is as if we are not submitting to God Himself.

But what about authorities who abuse their servants? Peter encourages the Christians in his first letter to *submit yourselves to your masters with all respect, not only to the good and gentle, but also to the cruel* (1 Pet. 2:18). Peter knew what harsh treatment was like; he lived during Nero's reign. If you are not familiar with Nero, he was a godless but powerful ruler in Rome. He hated Christians and delighted in persecuting them. Now, re-read 1 Peter 2:18, knowing that the cruel leaders were probably persecuting Christians. Peter was not condoning slavery. Instead he was preaching a principle that, when practiced, would ultimately destroy it.

How difficult would it be to submit to a godless ruler, knowing that your life could be on the line? On a scale of 1-10, rate your willingness to submit to this kind of leader.

1
no problem

5
maybe

10
no way

In 1 Peter 2:21, Peter tells us that we have a calling as Christians. Write that verse in the margin.

Jesus submitted to His authorities, and they killed Him! Just think, the very One who established the government and gave the authorities the right to rule had to submit to the evil and wickedness they perpetuated. Jesus left us a strong example. We should *follow in His steps* (v. 21).

In closing today, meditate on Proverbs 1:7 found in the margin. Not only is this verse the theme of the Book of Proverbs, but it is also a good guide for your life. Who holds Ultimately Authority over your life? Don't be a fool! Fear the Lord and gain knowledge.

The fear of the LORD is the beginning of knowledge; fools despise wisdom and instruction. (Prov. 1:7).

Day 4
Bring It Home

"Honor your father and mother—which is the first commandment with a promise—that it may go well with you and that you may have a long life in the land" (Eph. 6:2).

When God is established in your life and home, issues that seem complicated and difficult to resolve are simplified and settled. When His Word is seen as a revelation of His will, finding direction and making decisions for your life and family become a matter of seeking God's will as revealed by His Spirit through His Word.

What issues in your life and family seem difficult to resolve?
❑ balance of work and family time   ❑ discipline of children
❑ quality time with my spouse   ❑ quality time with the Lord
❑ other _____

Perhaps disciplining your children is difficult. Discipline is a necessary part of growth, both theirs and yours. Although they don't want to admit it, children want to know their limits and boundaries. Sometimes parents are tempted to discipline children out of anger. When our children "push our buttons," question our authority, or continue to rebel against the rules, we need to model how God disciplines us.

How do you respond when your authority is challenged?

How do you normally respond when your authority is challenged? If you have children, this may not be an uncommon experience! Think about how you normally respond. What is the outcome of doing discipline *your* way? Consider the following.

When God is the Ultimate Authority in your home, discipline communicates value and a sense of future possibility. It is measured with the knowledge that God is the audience and the One to whom a parent must give an account. Therefore, it must be approached in the same manner that God disciplines His children, with resolute determination and a full measure of grace.

How can the truths mentioned above change the way you deal with the discipline? The Bible has a lot to say about discipline. It often compares God's discipline of us as Christians to the discipline we give our children. Because God is our Ultimate Authority, He has the right (and obligation) to discipline us. We can learn this in the following verses.

Fill in the blanks of Hebrews 12:10b-11:

He [God] *does it for our _____, so that we can share His*
_____. No discipline seems _____ at the time,
but _____. Later on, however, it yields the
_____ and _____ to those
who have been trained by it.

As parents, we are our children's earthly authority, and we have the right (and obligation) to discipline them. But we must be careful to do it in the same manner and for the same reasons that God disciplines us.

You are probably familiar with the proverb: *"The one who will not use the rod hates his son, but the one who loves him disciplines him diligently"* (Prov. 13:24). Read other verses in Proverbs and list the reasons why it is important to discipline your children.

Why is it important to discipline your children?

22:6 _____

22:15 _____

23:13-14 _____

29:17 _____

When you establish in your home that God is the Ultimate Authority, respect for others, especially those in positions of authority, directly impacts our relationship with God. Refusing to honor a parent, for instance, is also refusing to honor God. This applies to a child of any age and parent.

Have you shown honor to your parents recently? If not, what will you do to honor them?

_____

_____

Settling the issue of God as the Ultimate Authority will also help you prioritize your affection for, or devotion to, God. The Scripture makes it clear that God is to be the first and foremost recipient of your devotion. After that, He will see to it that the others He brings into your life receive the love and devotion they need and deserve.

God's claim for first place in our hearts is justified.

God's claim for first place in our hearts is justified. After all, He says, *"I am the LORD your God, who brought you out of ... slavery"* (Ex. 20:2). In other words, He should be first in your heart because of His devotion to you and His deliverance of you. No wonder He refuses any other gods the privilege of receiving the slightest nod of affection from us!

How has God shown his devotion to you? Check all that apply. Add more to the list by writing them in the margin.
❏ my salvation ❏ a loving spouse
❏ good health ❏ Christian parents
❏ a job that provides for my family's financial needs
❏ other _____

Those in God's Kingdom Family understand that when we put God first in our devotion, He makes us channels through which His love is poured out to others. When I stand facing a young couple at the marriage altar, I remind them that there is no safer place for them in the heart of their husband or wife than second place, provided the Lord is in first place. God will see to our spouse's needs if He is allowed the place of Ultimate Authority in our heart. He also will see to the needs of our dearest friends. Answer the following statement honestly.

I believe someone other than God will meet all of my needs.
❏ True ❏ False

While the answer to this statement might seem obvious, you might act otherwise. But you know in your heart it is not their responsibility to fulfill a need only God can fill.

Take a few minutes to write in the margin a prayer of confession to God for the times that you don't acknowledge Him as your Ultimate Authority.

Also, go to others, if necessary, and confess the same to them. As a reminder to rely on God's faithfulness in meeting your needs, write Philippians 4:19 in the margin. Circle the words from this verse that encourage you the most.

Take a few minutes to read the verses in Ephesians 5, noting verse 32. Put yourself in the place of the Bride, and Christ in the place of the Groom. Read the verses again and record in the appropriate column how each is to respond to each other.

You are a part of the Bride. Christ is the Groom.

How Christ, the Groom, Loves Me	How I, the Bride, am to Love Christ
_____	_____
_____	_____
_____	_____
_____	_____
_____	_____

Pause to thank the Lord for the difference your relationship with Him has made in your life and in your family. Pray that those around you, especially your family members, will see Jesus in you.

Day 5
Relating to Others

"Whether you eat or drink, or whatever you do, do everything for God's glory" (1 Cor. 10:31).

Settling the issue of God being the Ultimate Authority will also affect those with whom you associate. This "one God" issue separated Israel from all of her neighbors. It became the standard applied to their marriages, their families, their relationships with other nations. This allegiance divided people from them and drew people to them.

Would people around you be surprised to hear that you believe in God?

❏ **yes**

❏ **no**

❏ **not sure**

How would those around you describe your allegiance to God?

❏ hot   ❏ cold   ❏ lukewarm

❏ bold   ❏ fearful   ❏ consistent

Read Deuteronomy 7:1-9. God told the Israelites not to make a treaty with seven nations. In addition, what else does God tell the Israelites *not* to do with the nations they will encounter?

_____

God tells them to do several things. Check each that applies.

❏ break down their altars   ❏ smash their sacred stones

❏ break down their Asherah poles   ❏ burn their idols in the fire

Throughout her history, God's judgment has fallen on Israel every time she has ignored this principle and adopted the worship and practices of other nations. Israel could have been faithful to God's covenant but she chose not to. Perhaps the people of Israel thought the risks were too high to follow God. Instead, they should have considered the risks of *not* following God.

Jesus was in the world yet not of the world, and He commands His Kingdom Family members to live in the same way (2 Cor. 6:14-18). If He had not possessed convictions that were different from those around Him, they would not have crucified Him. This is not a call to have a holier-than-thou attitude, nor is it a call to be weird. It *is* a call to be different.

Read Jesus' exhortation in Matthew 5:16. Check the following ways you can be different from the world but still be an effective witness of the gospel.

❑ be gentle in spirit with "difficult" family members
❑ visit a neighbor in the hospital or nursing home
❑ stay in your fenced back yard, hoping your neighbors will just ignore you
❑ take food and a card to a friend who just lost a loved one

Your faith also will make a difference in how you relate to other believers. You can read about this in Acts 2:42-47.

Read these verses. In the margin, write several things the believers did together.

Now, write the last part of verse 47. *And every day the Lord*

_____.

Their lives of singular and selfless devotion to the Lord literally drew others into the circle of His grace.

You have seen how settling the issue of God's authority will impact your associations and your affections. Now see how it will change your ambitions. Kingdom Family members who seek to love God above all and to express that love through obedience to Him will discover an impact on their ambitions. Love and devotion to God will change their behavior and their goals.

One of my longtime friends was a nightclub owner and professional gambler. When he came to Christ his ambitions changed radically. His live-in girlfriend, a dancer in his clubs, also came to know Christ just days afterward. I had the privilege of performing their wedding ceremony. Now they have a God-honoring family, and are faithful in their service to Him. My friend has answered God's call to the ministry, completed his seminary education, and is serving faithfully on a church staff. When God becomes the ultimate authority in our lives, He changes our ambitions!

When we put God in His rightful place of Ultimate Authority in our lives, some of our behavior changes direction 180 degrees. Perhaps this behavior isn't as dramatic as going from being a

Settling the issue of God's authority will also change your ambitions.

nightclub owner to a minister, but God did change the direction you were headed. What behavior in your life has changed drastically after you submitted to God's authority?

_____

What behavior/s still need to change? _____

_____

What specific reasons can you give God for not allowing the necessary changes to take place?

_____

Will you repent of your rebellion and submit to God as the established authority in your life? Write a prayer of confession, surrender, and gratitude for His grace.

_____

_____

Joseph's main concern was his relationship to God.

When you have come to grips with what it means to love God above all—to have no other gods before Him—your entire approach to life is affected. Consider Joseph who, under serious temptation by Potiphar's wife, said, *"How could I do such a great evil and sin against God?"* (Gen. 39:9). While conscious of his position and of his master's trust, Joseph's main concern was what this behavior would do to his relationship with a holy God whom he loved, trusted, and served.

God's initial commandment was stated in such a powerful form. *"Do not have other gods besides Me"* (Ex. 20:3). When this principle is established in your thinking, embraced in your heart, and endorsed by your behavior, you can fully enjoy what it means to be part of God's Kingdom family.

WEEK THREE

Respecting Human Life

"God created man in His own image; He created him in the image of God; He created them male and female" (Gen. 1:27).

I met the couple in the hallway of the hospital where I had been visiting with the husband's ailing mother. As we visited briefly, he expressed a concern I have heard on similar occasions. "Pastor, what do you think we should do with my mother?"

I am often asked this question, and I normally respond with the assurance of prayer as family members sort through the decisions they face. But on this occasion I was startled not so much by its substance as by the manner and tone in which it was asked. He could have been asking, "What do you think we should do with our old refrigerator? It doesn't work well, and it's in the way. You know, more of a nuisance than anything else. Got any good ideas? Can't just throw it away. At least, I'd rather not, anyway."

Day One
Created in God's Image

"God made man in His image" (Gen. 9:6).

In week one, you read an overview of pillar two. The Kingdom Family Commitment begins its look into this area by stating that "Human life is to be treasured, protected, encouraged, and loved from the moment of conception until the moment of death."

This week we will focus on what Scriptures have to say about this issue and how we can respond accordingly. Let's start at the beginning, with creation of the heavens, earth, and the first humans.

What was the difference between "good" and "very good"?

For five days, God had been creating the heavens and the earth (Gen. 1:1-25). He found everything to be *good*. But, in Genesis 1:31, we read that *"God saw all that He had made, and it was very good."* What made the difference?

Your Scripture verse for this week is Genesis 1:27. Write it below.

_____

_____

Your verse for today is Genesis 9:6. Write that latter part below.

_____

_____

Write a statement in the margin that expresses the similarities between these verses.

Yes, all of us are made in God's image. Does that mean that we *look* like Him physically? Jesus said that God is Spirit (John 4:24). Does it mean we act like Him? Only to the extent that He fills and rules over our lives.

Adam and Eve were created perfectly. They had no blemishes, no stains, no problems. God gave them a beautiful world to live in and to work in. Work wasn't a hindrance, but a joy. Then…

Adam and Eve were created perfectly. Then …

Enter the serpent. Genesis 3:1 says, *"The serpent was the _____ _____ of all the wild animals that the LORD God had made."*

The serpent was crafty. The woman was deceived. The man was deliberate. And sin entered the world. From that time, life has never been the same. At that moment, we became sinful.

The first child of the first parents committed murder. Read about this in Genesis 4:8-16. Verses 4 and 5 offer a hint at why Cain killed his brother, Abel. Write the reason below.

_____

Although Cain killed Abel, God protected Cain. *"Cain went out from the LORD's presence and lived in the land of Nod, east of Eden"* (Gen. 4:16).

From the moment of that original sin, our world has been cursed with sin and its ultimate expression: selfishness. Because of this, situations like the one we read about on the opening page this week are numerous. Also plaguing our society are the issues of abortion, child abuse, child molestation, pornography, and euthanasia. At the foundation of all of these issues is the lack of respect for human life. Life at every age has lost its value.

Read the following Scriptures that solidify the truth that life itself is a gift from God. Fill in the blanks where necessary.

Genesis 2:7: *"The _____ _____ formed the man out of the dust from the ground and breathed the breath of _____ into his nostrils, and the man became a living being."*

Job 33:4: *"The _____ ___ _____ has made me. And the breath of the _____ gives me life"* (NKJV).

Psalm 139:13: *"It was _____ who created my inward parts;*
_____ knit me together in my mother's womb."

The sin nature was passed on to all of us.

The sin nature of that original family was passed on to all of us. Because of this sinful nature, we must all pay a penalty. The Bible is very clear what the penalty is. Read the following verses and write beside each the word that best describes the penalty for sin.

Genesis 2:17 _____

Ezekiel 18:20 _____

Romans 6:23 _____

1 Corinthians 15:22 _____

But God did not leave us in a helpless situation. As much as we love our family members, we cannot do what it takes to save them. Psalm 49:7-8 says, *"These cannot redeem a person or pay his ransom to God—since the price of redeeming him is too costly, one should forever stop trying."*

To solve this dilemma, God sent us Jesus. Read Matthew 20:28 to discover that *just as the Son of Man did not come to be served, but to serve, and to give his life— _____ for many.*

Jesus was given as the ransom that we could not pay. That is how much God loves and respects human life. He loved us so much that He sent His only Son to redeem us to Himself (John 3:16).

If God has that much respect for all human life, how much should you respect that same life?

_____

_____

Today's study gave you a brief understanding of life as a gift. Pause to thank God for your life. Thank Him that you are made in His image. Thank God for His unconditional love that moved Him to send Jesus to pay the ransom for our sin.

Jesus was the ransom that we could not pay.

Day Two
From Conception to Death

"My bones were not hidden from You when I was made in secret, when I was formed in the depths of the earth. Your eyes saw me when I was formless; all my days were written in Your book and planned before a single one of them began" (Ps. 139:15-16).

Life "is to be treasured, protected, encouraged, and loved from the moment of conception until the moment of death."

The following verses talk about the various ages of life. Read them and select the appropriate response: Y = young; M = middle-aged; O = old. Some verses may refer to more than one age.

____ *"You are to rise in the presence of the elderly and honor the old. Fear your God; I am the LORD"* (Lev. 19:32).

____ *"Gray hair is a glorious crown; it is found in the way of righteousness"* (Prov. 16:31).

____ *"Grandchildren are the crown of the elderly, and the pride of sons is their fathers"* (Prov. 17:6).

____ *"The glory of young men is their strength, and the splendor of old men is gray hair"* (Prov. 20:29).

____ *"He will feed His flock like a shepherd; He will gather the lambs with His arm, and carry them in His bosom, and gently lead those who are with young"* (Isa. 40:11, NKJV).

____ *"No one should despise your youth; instead, you should be an example to the believers in speech, in conduct, in love, in faith, in purity"* (1 Tim. 4:12).

Review the story on page 43. This man's dilemma is common today. Longer, more healthy living, coupled with the astounding capabilities of modern medicine, have brought our society into uncharted territory. The term *sandwich generation* refers to the growing group of individuals who are confronted simultaneously with the responsibilities of rearing children, and sometimes grandchildren, while also tending to the growing needs of aging parents. The term is expressive, but it can be unfortunate if those in the middle of the sandwich ever began to consider themselves as more valuable to God than the others.

Are you in the middle of a sandwich?

Are you in the middle of a generational "sandwich?" If so, write your name and the names of the people you care for or who are dependent on you. If you aren't in this situation, think of someone who is and write their names below. After writing each name, take time to thank God for that person.

self: _____

spouse: _____

child/ren: _____

grandchild/ren: _____

parents: _____

The word *family* means many things today. No longer is family made up only of father, mother, and children. Several generations often live in one house; members can be blended, adopted, or fostered into one family. Then again, many family members live alone. Take a few minutes to answer the following questions about your family.

How are the senior adults in your family assured that their involvement is desired and valued?

_____

_____

How do the adults in your family show interest in the children?

_____

_____

How do the children in your family show parents, grandparents, and siblings a high level of respect?

_____

_____

Human life is a gift from God and must be treated as valuable regardless of one's age or physical condition. To do anything less is to assume a role God has reserved for Himself as Creator of life.

The psalmist David penned these words, declaring His humility toward God as his Creator.

It was You who created my inward parts;
You knit me together in my mother's womb.
I will praise You
because I am unique in remarkable ways.
Your works are wonderful,
and I know this very well.
My bones were not hidden from You
when I was made in secret,
when I was formed in the depths of the earth.
Your eyes saw me when I was formless;
all my days were written in Your book and planned
before a single one of them began (Ps. 139:13-16).

Circle the words in this passage that show respect for human life.

Jeremiah penned similar reflections: *"The word of the LORD came to me, saying: 'Before I formed you in the womb I knew you; before you were born I sanctified you' "* (Jer. 1:4-5, NKJV).

Life must be treated as a worthy gift from God.

Now it's your turn. Take the passage from Jeremiah and write your name in the blanks.

Before I formed _____ in the womb I knew
_____; before _____ [was] born
I sanctified _____.

Not only is God sovereignly involved in each person's conception, but He also has a specific role for each person to fulfill. God has each individual's welfare in mind.

God, you have searched me and you know me.

Read what David wrote about how intimately God knows you.

LORD, You have searched me and known me.
You know when I sit down and when I stand up;
You understand my thoughts from far away.
You observe my travels and my rest;
You are aware of all my ways (Ps. 139:1-3).

From what you have found in Scripture, what is God's view of the following issues?

Abortion _____

Euthanasia _____

Assisted suicide _____

Neglect of family members _____

Insensitivity to the plight of others _____

Indifference in sharing the gospel _____

Take a deep breath. Write a prayer in the margin, asking God to help you remember that He has a plan for you and everyone in your family. Ask God also to remind you that your responsibility is to seek His plan for you and then act within it.

Day Three
In the Later Years

"Gray hair is a glorious crown; it is found in the way of righteousness" (Prov. 16:31).

Much is being said and written these days about those who are in the later years of life and the choices facing them and their family members. It has become far too easy for those who are emotionally detached from a situation simply to decide that an individual must not be capable of enjoying the proper quality of life. Many senior adults are concerned about what will happen to them. And many confess to the silent fear of being cast off in a facility designed more for their death than their life. They know how easy it is for those who are out of sight soon to be out of mind.

Are you caring for an elderly loved one? ❑ yes ❑ no
If so, list this person's name in the margin.

Describe the situation.

**The person
I am caring
for is:**

_____

_____

Kingdom Family members know that God has the answer for this time in life as well. Whatever the answer, it will be consistent with the care God provides for His children.

David's 139th psalm continues to be instructive:
Where can I go to escape Your Spirit?
Where can I flee from Your presence?
If I go up to heaven, You are there;
if I make my bed in Sheol, You are there.
If I live at the eastern horizon
or settle at the western limits,
even there Your hand will lead me;
Your right hand will hold on to me.

If I say, "Surely the darkness will hide me,
and the light around me will become night"—
even the darkness is not too dark for You.
The night shines like the day;
darkness and light are alike to You (Ps. 139:7-12).

Where did David "find" God?

David didn't deny that being in the darkness was possible.
Have you experienced a period of darkness in the past few years?
❑ yes ❑ no   Describe the situation.

_____

_____

David learned throughout his years that God is present wherever
we are—loving and guiding us through any situation.

Carefully read the verses below that talk about God's presence.
Match the reference to the verse.

a. Psalm 51:11

___ " 'Am I a God near at hand,' says the LORD,
'and not a God afar off? Can anyone hide
himself in secret places, so I shall not see
him?' says the LORD. 'Do I not fill heaven
and earth?' says the LORD" (NKJV).

b. Isaiah 41:10

___ " 'Remember, I am with you always,
to the end of the age.' "

c. Jeremiah 23:23-24

___ "Do not banish me from Your presence
or take Your Holy Spirit from me."

d. Matthew 28:20

___ " 'Fear not, for I am with you; be not dis-
mayed, for I am your God. I will strength-
en you, yes, I will help you, I will uphold
you with My righteous right hand' "
(NKJV).

Whether found in the Old or New Testament, each of these
Scriptures reassure us of God's presence. In these situations,
God's presence was a positive reassurance. But read one more
verse. It comes from our friend Job. *"You put my feet in the stocks,*

and watch closely all my paths. You set a limit for the soles of my feet" (Job 13:27).

Does this comment sound like someone who is happy about having God with him? This may have been Job's way of saying, "I can't get by with anything! You are always aware of my situation and my response." In fact, Job's statement about the marks on the soles of his feet are a reference to the practice of masters who not only put their servant's feet in shackles, but also branded them so that others would know whose servants were theirs.

In what situation would we not want God watching us?

_____

_____

Thankfully, God doesn't watch over His children like a cruel master watching over a slave. God watches over us to protect us, to guide us. He watches over us because He loves us.

By God's grace, an individual's usefulness increases with age until the moment God calls us home. My mother lay comatose in a hospital bed for several weeks before her death. Each of her children has since shared that at some point, when alone with her in that bedside vigil, they made some significant decisions in light of her imminent death—decisions motivated by her love for us and the strength of her character. Her utility for God increased right up to the moment of her death.

If usefulness to God is sustained until the moment of our death, then we should care for our family members with that in view.

Recently I visited in the home of a senior adult couple as they celebrated their sixtieth wedding anniversary. The house was packed with loving church and family members. Long ago some might have suggested that the bride of sixty years should be placed in a care center. That day might come, in fact. And if it does, her

God watches over us because He loves us.

53

family will proceed with love, attentiveness, care, and dignity. Her husband said to me with tears one day, "I'm enjoying fulfilling *this* part of my marriage vow."

Instead of thinking of his life's comforts, this man has given himself to caring for other family members at crucial times. In the end he will discover that in the process he was fulfilling God's great design for his life as well. He was becoming like his Master.

One of last things King David did was to "charge" his son Solomon. Read 1 Kings 2:1-12. Check what David challenged his son to do.
❑ Be strong.
❑ Observe what the Lord your God requires.
❑ Walk in the Lord's ways.
❑ Keep the Lord's decrees and commands.

How will you charge your children to live?

Will you follow David's example? How will you charge your children to live? Take a few minutes to think about what you would like to say to your children to pass on your legacy. What legacy of faith will you leave them?

Day Four
Show Genuine Interest

" 'Son,' he said to him, 'you are always with me, and everything I have is yours' " (Luke 15:31).

Have you grasped the significance of the infinite value God places on all human life, His intimate knowledge of us, and His intense concern for our welfare? If so, you should think seriously about how you will respond to your own family members in the various stages of their life's pilgrimage.

If God values us infinitely, you should communicate to each of your family members how much you value them and your relationship with them. Let me introduce you to a family who models this.

This couple has adopted and are rearing their granddaughter who has disabilities because of a parent's drug use. Severely impaired at birth and neglected by her own mother, this young girl was destined to spend the balance of her life in an institution. But she was rescued by her grandparents and has, by their testimony, contributed more to them than they ever imagined contributing to her.

What family member has contributed more to you than you have contributed to them?

_____

In what way has he or she made this contribution to your life?

_____

We all need others who care about our welfare. God has a passionate interest in us. In the parable of the prodigal son, the father sees his wayfaring son at a distance and runs to meet him. Later the same father goes out to talk with the pouting older brother.

You will find this amazing story in Luke 15:11-32. Read it and answer the following questions by marking T (*True*) or F (*False*).
___ The father gave up all hope that his son would ever return.
___ The younger son didn't think of restoration, only a good job.
___ The father's joy was unrestrained.
___ The older son felt slighted.
___ The older son realized that steady obedience had its reward.
___ The father dealt with each son according to his nature.

Who is the hero in this story? _____

Why? _____

_____

God has a passionate interest in us.

The father showed genuine interest in both sons. He didn't show favoritism to either the one who strayed or the one who stayed. Of

55

all the positive things the father did, which would be most difficult for you to do in a similar situation? Choose from the following:

❏ meet your younger son before he headed up the driveway
❏ forgive the younger son without rehearsing his sins
❏ throw a party and invite everyone
❏ deal with the older son in an understanding way

Jesus told this parable to illustrate how deep and impartial God's love is to all of His children. Luke 15:31 gives the father's response to the older son when he complained about being slighted. Fill in the blanks of that verse below.

"You are _____ with me, and _____ I have is yours."

Now, personalize this verse by writing your name below.
_____ is always with me, and everything I have is _____.

Are you most like the prodigal or the older son?

Which of the father's sons most closely describes you and your behavior?

❏ the prodigal son   ❏ the older son   ❏ both

Explain your answer._____

_____

How has your Heavenly Father responded when you have turned away from Him?

_____

_____

How does He respond when you turn your face toward home?

_____

Just as the father in this story had to celebrate because of his son's return home, God celebrates when His wayward children return to Him in confession and repentance.

Our interest in the welfare of others should be prompted by God's interest in us. We turn again to Psalm 139 to find David's words revealing.

God, how difficult Your thoughts are for me to comprehend;
how vast their sum is!
If I counted them, they would outnumber the grains of sand;
when I wake up, I am still with You (Ps. 139:17-18).

Do each of your family members know that you are similarly interested in their welfare? ❏ yes   ❏ no

How are you communicating your interest, love, and concern for each member of your family?

When does God stop being interested in you and your welfare?

Take time to thank God for His never-ending attention and interest in your welfare. Ask Him to create within you a similar heart of concern for the welfare of each member of your family.

Day Five
Initiate and Inspire
"Since I am persuaded of this, I know that I will remain and continue with all of you for your advancement and joy in the faith" (Phil. 1:25).

Paul writes, "I'm in a bind. I desire to die and be with Christ, and that would be best. But right now it's more necessary for me to stick around and help you. So that's what I will do. I will stay, spend time with you, and help you grow and rejoice in your faith" (Phil. 1:23-25, my paraphrase).

Paul was opening a discussion on a subject that was on the minds of many who refused to discuss it for "propriety's sake." No one really likes to talk about difficult situations. Especially situations involving those who are ill, or facing imminent death, or in need of extended and special care. We tend to turn our conversations to happier times. But, if you haven't yet, you will probably face a time when you must make difficult decisions that affect your family.

As you consider your responsibilities to your family, which ones are, or will soon be, difficult to resolve?

_____

Do these involve the physical welfare of a family member (aging, physical disabilities, etc.)? ❑ yes   ❑ no

Are you the one primarily assigned the responsibility of resolving the issue? ❑ yes   ❑ no

How is the rest of your family involved in making this decision?

_____

_____

Are you the one responsible for resolving the issue?

Prayerfully, and with counsel, choose an appropriate time and place to gather those together who need to be involved in making the decision. Be sure to express a godly love and kindness toward each family member and the one/s to whom you are referring.

Recently, an ailing family matriarch turned to me in the presence of her children and grandchildren and said, "Pastor, when I die, I'd like to be stuffed and mounted over the kitchen table. That way they'll know I'm still watching what they eat and listening to what they say!" Her humor took the edge off what she knew was a difficult moment for her children. It was another way of communicating her concern for them.

God is intensely concerned for the welfare of every member of your family, including you. His concern, in fact, was ultimately illustrated by sending His Son who gave His life for us. Writing of this event, the apostle Paul said:

Make your attitude that of Christ Jesus, who, existing in the form of God, did not consider equality with God as something to be used for His own advantage. Instead He emptied Himself by assuming the form of a slave, taking on the likeness of men. And when He had come as a man in His external form, He humbled Himself by becoming obedient to the point of death—even to death on a cross. For this reason God also highly exalted Him and gave Him the name that is above every name, so that at the name of Jesus every knee should bow—of those who are in heaven and on earth and under the earth—and every tongue should confess that Jesus Christ is Lord, to the glory of God the Father (Phil. 2:5-11).

Make your attitude for your family like that of Christ.

Your concern for your family should be modeled after Christ's concern for you. Your attentiveness, sensitivity, and faithfulness will inspire others to follow your example. Read through the passage again and answer the following questions thoughtfully.

Did Christ make a difficult decision with His own advantage in mind? ❏ yes ❏ no

Did He feel that He was the only one whose interest was at stake? ❏ yes ❏ no

Did Christ distance Himself emotionally and physically from the ones in need? ❏ yes ❏ no

Did Christ establish specific limits on His involvement in our need? ❏ yes ❏ no

While every difficult situation is different, your answers to the questions above can serve as a guide to your thinking.

Close by praying, thanking God for knowing and loving you even before you were born.

Exercising Moral Purity

"As the One who called you is holy, you also are to be holy in all your conduct; for it is written, 'Be holy, because I am holy' " (1 Pet. 1:15-16).

While waiting for the departure of a flight, I could not help but notice a seedy-looking, older man who clutched a brown sack tightly in his hand. I thought to myself, *That guy's got some booze in the sack. After we board the flight, he'll start hitting his own private bottle. How sad to see the toll his addiction has taken on his life—physically, spiritually, and morally.*

After being seated on the plane, I noticed the same man sitting opposite but one row forward of me. I settled back to see how long it would before he hit the bottle. Imagine my surprise when, after somewhat secretly glancing around to see if anyone was watching, he pulled out, not a liquor bottle, but a pornographic magazine. This man's life had been burned up in his pursuit of youthful lust.

Day One
Start at Home

*"A man's ways are before the LORD's eyes, and He considers
all his paths"* (Prov. 5:21).

As a member of God's Kingdom Family, you hold to the truths
of God's written Word and seek to apply those truths to your life.
You desire to be faithful and pure before the Lord.

This week we look at pillar three. We will look at how this area
affects both you and your family. If you have more than one member in your family, first put your own life under a spiritual micro-
scope. If you are the head of your household, your responsibility is
to make sure that you are faithful and pure. Next, you are responsible to teach those under your authority. As in all cases, communicating the importance of moral purity requires personal example,
precept, and firm purpose of heart. The Adversary's attack in this
area is both open and secret. You must pray for wisdom, protection, and loving discernment.

Pray for wisdom, protection, and loving discernment.

Take time now to look inward. Read aloud this prayer from Psalm
139:23-24 as you dedicate yourself to faithfulness and purity.

Search me, God, and know my heart;
test me and know my concerns.
See if there is any offensive way in me;
lead me in the everlasting way.

Pillar three in the Family Commitment reads:
God has established the family as His first institution on earth. It is
worthy of my most noble aspirations and commitments, including my
commitment to moral purity, marital fidelity, and Christ-like love for
each family member. Because marriage is a picture of Christ's faith-
fulness to His bride, the church, and because the family is a picture of
the Father's faithfulness to His children, I will honor the Lord by being
faithful and pure.

Before you continue with your study today, circle words or phrases that are most meaningful to you in pillar three.

Remember that God has established the home as a sacred institution.

Throughout this workbook you will be reminded that God has established the home as a sacred institution. Properly understood, it is to be where a person's spiritual pilgrimage begins and subsequently is formed.

Did you learn about Jesus in your home as a child? If so, write about that experience.

_____

_____

Was the importance of moral purity effectively communicated in your home? Tell about this.

_____

_____

What about your home now? Give one example of how Jesus' presence is so welcome that He's considered part of the family.

_____

_____

If you are not in a home where biblical principles are lived and taught, then can ask God to help you to be the first in line of a new generation of God-fearing and Christ-honoring people. Mark in the margin today's date as a commitment to be the first in your family to follow and honor Jesus.

In addition to what God has said about the sanctity of the home, He commands each member of His Kingdom Family to live a life of personal holiness (1 Pet. 1:15-16). Such a life is an absolute contradiction to what our society communicates as being normal, natural, and even healthy.

Write 1 Peter 1:15-16 in the margin.

How can we be holy in our world?
❏ Implement the truths of the seven pillars in our life and family.
❏ Read the Word to help us know right and wrong in God's eyes.
❏ Flee from anything that is intended to incite lust.
❏ Find a few Christlike friends who will hold us accountable.

We might think that we are holy and pure as long as we appear that way to others. That's not the case, according to Jesus. *"The Lord said to him: 'Now you Pharisees clean the outside of the cup and dish, but inside you are full of greed and evil' "* (Luke 11:39).

Which statement below most accurately describes your concern?
❏ I am most concerned about what I am inwardly before God.
❏ I am most concerned about how I appear before others.

Our culture has embraced the art of compartmentalization. That's a long word that says that "My private life is private. It has no effect on what kind of person I am or how I do my job."

Unfortunately, we have seen this false belief fleshed out in politics, business, and even in the church. You've heard the term "Sunday Christian." This describes a person who attends worship on Sunday but doesn't attend to the faithful exercise of Christian character or discipline the other six days of the week.

Look at your Scripture verse for today. Write it below.

_____

_____

Let's break it into two parts: *in full view* and *examines all his paths. A man's ways are in full view of the* LORD.

"My private life has no effect on what kind of person I am."

Match the verse with the reference.

a. Job 31:4 _____ *"The eyes of the LORD are everywhere, observing the wicked and the good."*

b. Proverbs 15:3 _____ *"My eyes are on all their ways; they are not hidden from My face, nor is their iniquity hidden from My eyes"* (NKJV).

c. Jeremiah 16:17 _____ *"Does He not see my ways, and count all my steps?"* (NKJV).

God is a loving and caring Father, not a "Big Brother."

In George Orwell's book *1984,* Big Brother constantly was watching over the people, checking to see if what they were doing was against the government. God is not Big Brother! Instead, He is a loving and caring Father, watching the actions of His children, wanting them to love Him and share His love with others.

He examines all his paths.
In Psalm 26, David challenges God to examine his ways. Fill in the blanks where appropriate in these verses.

Test me, LORD, and try me; _____ my heart and mind.
I do not sit with the _____ or associate with _____.
I _____ a crowd of evildoers, and I do not sit with the _____.
I wash my hands in _____ and go around Your altar,
LORD, raising my voice in _____ and telling about
Your _____ _____ (Ps. 26:2,4-7).

David was not professing to live a perfect life. But, his desire was to be above reproach. He wanted God to be able to test him at any time and find him obedient.

Let's get personal. Since Proverbs 5:21 is a settled fact, how pleased is God with your daily moral choices? Plot where you are.

displeased   depends on whether I   pleased
                              remember and care that
                              He's looking

What moral practices or habits have you adopted that hinder your relationship with God?

_____

_____

How do these affect your family?

_____

_____

How do they impact the effectiveness of your witness to others?

_____

_____

What are some positive steps you can take each day as indications of your desire to live a holy life?
❑ Read from the Bible daily.
❑ Memorize verses about specific issues.
❑ Ask for accountability from a trusted friend.
❑ Spend time in prayer, dedicating myself daily to follow the Lord's ways.
❑ other _____

Holiness springs from the heart! It must be within the heart that we establish our intentions to be morally pure and maritally faithful, expressing Christlike love for each member of our family. Ask God to give you the grace to live a life of genuine holiness and moral purity.

Day Two
Reach Forward

"I do not consider myself yet to have taken hold of it [the goal]. But one thing I do: forgetting what is behind and reaching forward to what is ahead, I pursue as my goal the prize promised by God's heavenly call in Christ Jesus" (Phil. 3:13-14).

Ask God to give you grace to live a life of genuine holiness and moral purity.

Decide to set your moral compass in the right direction before times of testing.

The intended purpose of this chapter is to move you toward both a commitment to and the practice of moral purity, marital faithfulness, and Christlike love for each member of your family. You should not wait until you have come to a moral crossroad before making this decision. You should arrive at such a time of testing with your moral compass already set in the right direction.

If you have made sinful moral choices, admit that you have. You don't need to write them down. You know what they are, and most importantly, God knows what they are. Confess these choices and ask God to help you turn your life's direction toward one that is positive and God-honoring. Pray something like this: "Lord, according to 1 John 1:9, You've promised that if I confess my sins, You are faithful to forgive me of my sins and to cleanse me from all unrighteousness. Please forgive me of the poor moral choices I've made. I want to be righteous like You. I want to make better moral choices."

According to James 1:5, *"If anyone lacks wisdom, he should ask God, who gives to all generously and without criticizing, and it will be given to him."* Lord, please guide me in the right direction and give me the wisdom and grace to stay on the right path. Thank You for Your grace, mercy, and love that covers me. Amen.

You've just taken a very positive step in the right direction! But, confessing does not mean that the earthly consequences of your sin will suddenly disappear or that God will remove all consequences of previous mistakes. Let's take a look at a moment in Israel's history that reminds us that sin has consequences.

You will find this story in Numbers 20:1-13. The Israelites were complaining … again. They quarreled with Moses about several things, but especially over their desire for water. Moses and his brother Aaron went to *"the tent of meeting. They fell down with their faces to the ground, and the glory of the LORD appeared to them"* (v. 6).

What did the Lord say next to Moses and Aaron, found in verse 8? Check all that apply on the next page.

❏ Take your staff.   ❏ Go alone, don't take Aaron.
❏ Gather the assembly.   ❏ Speak to the rock before the
                                                          people.

In an earlier and similar experience with Israel (Ex. 17:5-6), God had told Moses to strike the rock a single time. I believe this was to be a picture of the effect of our Lord's crucifixion, and its sufficiency in providing the water of life.

Now, on this second occasion, was Moses supposed to strike the rock? _____

Instead, how did Moses respond (v. 11)? _____

God provided water, but He also saw that Moses did not honor Him in front of the people. Moses had failed to illustrate by his obedience the simple fact that Christ's crucifixion was sufficient, once for all. Sadly, the Lord said to Moses and Aaron, " *'Because you did not trust Me to show My holiness in the sight of the Israelites, you will not bring this assembly into the land I have given them'* " (v. 12).

How devastating! Moses longed to enter the Promised Land and to see God's people live in freedom. Yet his sin kept him from seeing the promise fulfilled. His sad experience is a reminder that God's work must be done God's way. I insert this story here because many are under the impression that they can "sow wild oats" and then, through the simple act of confession, escape the privilege of reaping them. All you can do with sin, however, is either live in it, or repent of it. You don't have the choice of avoiding its consequences.

As you close your study, review today's Scripture verse. Paul reminds us that the secret is in *"forgetting what is behind and reaching forward to what is ahead"* (Phil. 3:13).

The past is the past. A friend of mine said that she wants to remember her past enough not to repeat it but forget it enough to move forward. How will you move forward this week?

All you can do with sin is either live in it, or repent of it.

Day Three
Get into the Word

"How can a young man keep his way pure? By keeping Your word" (Ps. 119:9).

For the rest of this week, you will explore four specific practices that will help you to remain faithful and pure before God.

Fill your heart with the Word of God. By doing this, you first experience a dynamic cleansing of your thoughts. " *'You are already clean because of the word I have spoken to you,'* " said Jesus to His disciples on the eve of His crucifixion (John 15:3). In this verse, *the word* means the audible words that Jesus spoke to His disciples. For us, it means the written Word.

God's Word cleans out and replaces the evil thoughts in our hearts.

Here Christ is speaking of more than mere positive thinking. He is saying that His Word actually cleans out and replaces the evil thoughts that have lodged in our hearts.

Read the following verse. Based on what you read, how does God use the Bible to perform "heart surgery?"

Hebrews 4:12 _____

When we faithfully approach the Word we receive renewed thinking, protection, and guidance. Three verses in Psalm 119 frame the outline for these three remarkable benefits of reading God's Word. In the space below each verse write in a personal example of the way God's Word has provided help for you in that specific area.

Renewed thinking: *"How can a young man keep his way pure? By keeping Your word"* (v. 9).

_____

Protection: *"I have treasured Your word in my heart so that I may not sin against You"* (v. 11).

_____

Guidance: *"Your word is a lamp for my feet and a light on my path"* (v. 105).

What place does the prayerful reading of God's Word have in your daily life? Place an "X" on the spot that best fits where you are today. Be honest! Remember, no one will see your answer; this is between you and God.

no place   I like to read God's Word when I have a question   I do not go a day without reading God's Word

How long as it been since, by reading the Bible, you have become convicted of a specific sin, confessed, repented, and gained victory over it?

❏ a few days   ❏ a few weeks
❏ several months   ❏ several years
❏ I haven't ever been convicted by reading the Bible

Do you find that specific Scriptures come to mind when you are being tempted to sin? If so, list some of them in the margin.

These Scriptures help when I am being tempted to sin:

When Solomon said to his son, *"Guard your heart above all else, for it is the source of life"* (Prov. 4:23), he was pointing to a practical manner in which his son could live out the truths quoted in these psalms. "Guard your heart (your mind, will, emotions). Be careful what you put into it, for it is from your heart that you establish the boundaries of your life!" What better resource for establishing your life's boundaries—and your goals—than the pure Word of God.

Day Four
Lust vs. Holy Living

"God has not called us to impurity, but to sanctification" (1 Thess. 4:7).

Today we will look at two more practices that will help you remain faithful and pure before God. Perhaps these are the two that most often come to mind when you are thinking about a life of moral purity and marital fidelity.

Paul's instruction to Timothy, and to us, on the issue of moral purity is clear. Write out 2 Timothy 2:22 in the margin.

Lust—a strong, unholy passion—is brought to the surface when we give way to temptation. Paul exhorted Timothy to *flee from youthful passions,* knowing that they can quickly become so imbedded in our character that they guide behavior for the balance of life.

Check several words that define lust.
❏ passion   ❏ desire
❏ love   ❏ greed
❏ sin   ❏ other _____

We aren't told if Timothy had a problem with a lustful heart. But because Timothy was a leader in the church in Ephesus, Paul wanted him to set a good example for others.

Paul wanted Timothy to set a good example.

Write out Paul's exhortation to the church found in Colossians 3:5.

_____

_____

In this verse Paul equates lust, and its associates, with _____.

Who is the "idol" being worshiped when these practices are prevalent in your life?
❏ Satan?   ❏ Self?
❏ Sex, or a sexual partner? ❏ Other?_____

The practices Paul refers to stem from our old, earthly nature. Read the promise we are given in 2 Corinthians 5:17: *"If anyone is in Christ, he is a new creation; old things have passed away, and look, new things have come!"* We might struggle with lust even as we are being renewed day by day. Yet, the Bible is clear about what we are to do: Put these things to death! Deliberately consider them judged as evil and take them to the cross! These practices are not consistent with who you are anymore!

Take a break and get ready for some exciting news!

God wants you to set your heart on His plan for your life and marriage (Col. 3:2) To "set" means to focus your attention or affections on something. God says that His plan is the one that should attract our attention and affections.

When God first began speaking to my heart regarding marriage, I prayed that He would give me direction in His Word. He gave me the entire fifth chapter of Ephesians as a pattern for the relationship I should have with my future wife. Negatives were to be avoided and positives were to be accepted. For me, that pattern became the standard that I would hold up as I considered a future mate. Soon I met my future wife who, by conviction and character, fulfilled the description of Ephesians 5. God had graciously given me that passage so that I might set my heart upon it.

Ephesians 5 provides a wonderful picture of the relationship that exists between Christ (the Groom) and the Church (the Bride). But the chapter also contains practical instructions about the relationship that should exist between every married couple.

Read Ephesians 5 carefully and answer the following questions:

(vv. 1-2) Who are we to imitate? _____

How are we to walk? _____

(vv. 3-14) How are the children of darkness described?

_____

God wants you to set your heart on His plan for your life.

How are the children of light described? _____

Which set of descriptions most nearly characterizes you?

_____

(vv. 15-21) How are the unwise described? _____

How are the wise described? _____

(vv. 22-33) What are the responsibilities of a husband?

_____

What are the responsibilities of a wife?

_____

This kind of life is possible for you!

The exciting news is that this kind of life is possible for you! Ephesians 5:18b explains the way you can live by God's pattern. Write the command in the margin.

Someone has said, "If you don't know where you're going, any path will get you there." Of course, there's the problem! God doesn't want us traveling "any path." He has a divinely conceived plan for us, a plan He is willing to reveal to those willing to search it out. Prayerfully surrender to the Lordship of Christ and claim His promise of continued filling with the Holy Spirit. Ask Him to guide you in your life, your marriage, and your family relationships.

Day Five
Find a Friend

"Iron sharpens iron, and one man sharpens another" (Prov. 27:17).

A final way to establish a life of faithfulness and purity is to get help. Really! Find a trustworthy friend and become accountable.

If you are married, this person will probably be your life's mate. However, you may choose a close friend (of the same gender) who is willing to provide this kind of encouragement. Regardless of who it is, you must be willing to let him or her ask you life's difficult questions.

Among your earthly relationships, who is holding you accountable? Write this person's name in the margin.

Thank God now for this person. Ask God to give this person genuine discernment.

Read your Scripture for today. After you read it, rub your hands together as if each hand were a piece of iron mentioned. Notice the friction? Friction is necessary if rough places are to become smooth, or sharp.

Who sharpens you like this? Write their name in the margin.

If you do not have someone to encourage you and hold you accountable, stop now to ask God for such a person. Perhaps someone is looking for a person like you to encourage them and hold them accountable.

One of the most unique examples in the Bible of an encourager is Barnabas. We first meet Barnabas in Acts 4:36. There we read about *Joseph, who was named by the apostles Barnabas, which is translated Son of Encouragement.*

Most likely, Barnabas received this name from the apostles because of his positive response to a stranger. Acts 9:27 tells us about this man. What was his name? _____

Paul certainly needed a friend, and he definitely needed encouragement! In an act of faith and courage, Barnabas met Paul at a neutral place, and he actually took Paul to meet with the apostles. Paul had formerly been seeking out Christians to have them put to death. God put it in Barnabas's heart to believe Paul's story. Later,

Barnabas joined Paul as he began to minister in various cities.

When the church at Antioch was in its infancy, several Christian men knew who to send for as they tried to encourage the people. Fill in the blanks of Acts 11:23-24 what was said about Barnabas.

When he arrived and saw the grace of God, he was glad, and he _____ all of them to _____ _____ to the Lord with a firm resolve of the heart—for he was a _____ _____, full of the Holy Spirit and of faith—and large numbers were added to the Lord.

Not only was Barnabas an encouragement to the Christians in Antioch, he also helped to share the good news of eternal encouragement so that others came to know Jesus as he knew Him.

How has your encourager helped you recently?

_____

How did you respond?

_____

We all need encouragement in our Christian walk.

Although we all need encouragement in our Christian walk, we don't necessarily need someone to condone our actions. Especially if those actions are contrary to what God has for our lives.

Several years ago I read a book titled *The Man Who Could Do No Wrong.* The book chronicled a dismal period in the life of a pastor. In describing the events that led to the collapse of his ministerial empire, the author observed that one of his fatal mistakes was in surrounding himself with men who were complimentary of him rather than complementary to him. With the difference of only one vowel in the spelling, the words mean totally different things. In the first instance, one finds men who were simply "rubber stamps" for his position on virtually anything. Telling him the sky was the limit, they flattered his ego and thus, unwittingly, laid a snare for his feet. Had he chosen the latter instead, he would have been surrounded by men who challenged him, causing him to think through the potential consequences of his actions. These men would not have tolerated any compromise of character.

To help you maintain a life of moral purity you don't need a clone but a loving critic, someone whose advice you are willing to heed, someone you respect, someone who will be your greatest ally— and your greatest adversary if you adopt destructive moral practices. Ask God to help you find just such a person.

Read 2 Samuel 12:2. God put such a man in the life of King David; a man who would confront him regarding his sin of adultery. What was that man's name?

What was David's response?

_____

Now read verse 13. In the margin, write David's response to the man whom God had sent to hold him accountable.

Ask God to bring the right person (or people) into your life to hold your accountable. Read again the verse for the day and tell the Lord you want to be a sharp instrument for His use whatever the cost.

When God gives you the name of that person, write it below.

_____

The world is full of dismal statistics regarding crumbling marriages and moral failure, but you don't need to be one of them. Determine now that you will honor the family, God's first institution, with a life of moral purity and marital fidelity. Purpose to live a holy and godly life. And guard your heart, filling it with the Word of God, fleeing enticements to sin against God and your family, fixing your vision on His plan for your life, and finding a genuine accountability partner.

Serving My Church

"I rejoiced with those who said to me, 'Let us go to the house of the LORD*' "* (Ps. 122:1).

Recently I received a letter from a young woman in our singles ministry, asking prayer as she began a new route in our bus ministry. In the letter she shared that she was a product of our church's outreach to students. She spoke of a home situation that included an absent father, an unsaved mother, and a string of abuses. She recalled how, prior to meeting Christ, she often had thoughts of suicide. But all of that changed when she came to know Jesus as Lord and Savior. Now she had a burden for children like herself; children who needed the transforming touch of Christ. No one was twisting her arm to get her involved in reaching out to others through her church. She had been praying for the opportunity.

Day One
What Is the Church?

"I have written so that you will know how people ought to act in God's household, which is the church of the living God, the pillar and foundation of the truth" (1 Tim. 3:15).

Ask people to describe *church*, and you will hear a variety of answers. For some, church is more of a favorite place than a fellowship of people. For others, the association between church and a specific place is never made because they meet in a variety of locations. Still others will tell you that church is their life and all their activities revolve around the events on the schedule for each week. Of course, for some, church is reserved for special days and occasions.

What is *church* to you?
- ❏ the people
- ❏ the building and the people
- ❏ other _____
- ❏ the building
- ❏ a place for special occasions

What is church to you?

The church is the bride of Christ, comprised of all the redeemed who will, one day, be caught up to heaven to spend eternity with Him. In the meantime, we realize that each church is the local representation of the body of Christ. Church members are each uniquely gifted by the Spirit of God so that, in fellowship together, their community can experience Christ at work among them. The local church is worthy of faithful attendance, diligent service, generous and God-honoring giving, and loving cooperation.

Are you a member of a local church? ❏ yes ❏ no

If so, give the name of your church. _____

Read 1 Timothy 3:15 again. What words did Paul use to describe the church in this verse?

_____

As we talk about the Kingdom Family in this workbook, do you find it interesting that Paul refers to the church as God's household? Look up the following verses and note the common reference to the church.

Psalm 122:1 _____

Matthew 21:13 _____

John 2:16 _____

Just as each of your family members has a unique set of gifts, skills, and abilities, so every member in God's Kingdom Family has gifts. When Paul was writing to the Ephesians, he talked about each of us having different gifts. Turn to this passage in chapter 4, verse 11, and fill in each gift.

He personally gave some to be _____, *some* _____, *some* _____, *some* _____ *and* _____.

The church could not function if we all had the same gift.

Could the church function if we all had the same gift? Not very well. In fact, not at all.

Again, Paul talks about different gifts and functions in 1 Corinthians 12:12-25. He uses the analogy of a body to explain the various gifts present in a local church. Check from the following list the parts of the body to which Paul compares the body of Christ.

❏ foot   ❏ hand   ❏ feet
❏ ear   ❏ eye   ❏ head
❏ nose (sense of smell)

According to these verses, are any parts better than another?
❏ yes   ❏ no

Some might be weaker, some stronger; some more honorable, some less honorable. But, all of the parts are important. That's not to say that all parts of the body function adequately or perfectly, though. The reason Paul wrote his letter to Timothy is found in the first part of 1 Timothy 3:15. In the margin describe Paul's reason for writing.

Every age has suffered its share of ecclesiastical embarrassments. In fact, some have chosen to write off the church as an absurd idea. "After all," they say, "look at the hypocrites!"

Have you heard anyone describe the church as "a bunch of hypocrites"? ❏ yes ❏ no

If so, to what were they referring:
❏ a specific event ❏ a person
❏ a local body ❏ churches in general
❏ other _____

Yes, you can find hypocrites in the church. But you also will find ordinary men and women who seek to follow the Lord faithfully. Remember that the church is built upon Christ in whom there has never been, nor ever will be, the slightest compromise of integrity. However, Christ has chosen to build His Church using imperfect people. We disappoint one another, let each other down, fall into temptation. The bottom line is that we are sinners.

Pause to thank God for allowing you to be part of His household, the church. Ask Him for strength to use the gifts He has given you to fulfill the role He has for you.

Day Two
The Chief Cornerstone

" 'This [Jesus] is the stone despised by you builders, who has become the cornerstone' " (Acts 4:11).

Take a trip with me back to the days immediately following Christ's ascension. Jerusalem is buzzing with news of the incredi-

The Jewish community has been turned upside down.

ble events of Pentecost. The church in Jerusalem is expanding exponentially. The Jewish community, along with its leadership, has been turned upside down and is in a defensive mode. Now word has reached them of a miracle. A man, lame from birth, has been healed. A crowd has gathered in the outer court and Peter is preaching, this time emphasizing Christ's resurrection. The Sadducees, longtime foes of the resurrection, take matters into their own hands and have Peter and John arrested.

Although the religious leaders were opposing what Peter and John were saying, according to Acts 4:4, how did the people respond? Mark each statement T (*True*) or F (*False*).

____ The people heard and believed.

____ The people supported the religious leaders in having Peter and John arrested.

____ The people got scared when Peter and John were arrested.

____ The number of men who believed the gospel message was about 5,000.

After a night in jail, Peter and John now find themselves standing before the council. Annas, the high priest, Caiaphas, John and Alexander, and all the members of the high-priestly family asked Peter a question.

Read Peter's answer in Acts 4:10. List the credentials of the One in whose name Peter and John healed the lame man.

_____

In addition to these powerful credentials, Peter offers this important commentary: " *'This [Jesus] is the stone despised by you builders, who has become the cornerstone'* " (4:11).

Peter's audience was not made up of construction workers, but they were familiar with what he said.
The stone that the builders rejected
has become the cornerstone (Ps. 118:22).
At this time, a building was constructed by first laying the corner-

stone. Everything was built on that stone; it anchored the building. All other stones were placed in relation to it. That stone became the standard by which all was measured in the building. Furthermore, it was not uncommon for the chief cornerstone to join together the two most important, or load bearing, walls in the building.

Now read Ephesians 2:20.

The wall of the Old Testament is built on the _____.

The wall of the New Testament is built on the _____.

Who is the cornerstone, tying these two walls together? _____

The cornerstone was the standard by which all was measured.

Perhaps you have seen modern versions of a cornerstone. They are usually placed after a building is completed and record the name of its builders and owners, and the date of completion.

Use the box below to write your name and the date that Jesus became your Chief Cornerstone. You might also want to include the names of those who helped you come to Christ, along with an important Scripture verse.

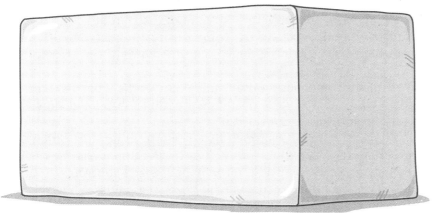

Thank God for sending His Son Jesus to be your cornerstone.

Day Three
The Only Message

" 'There is salvation in no one else, for there is no other name under heaven given to people by which we must be saved' " (Acts 4:12).

Occasionally I hear someone lament how difficult it is for them to share their faith with others.

Do you find it easy or difficult to share the gospel? Mark an "X" where you are on the line below.

```
|_____|_____|_____|_____|_____|_____|
```

very difficult   depends on   comfortable in
                        who it is   most situations

In reality, the gospel message is bigger than any difficulty we might encounter to share it. People scarcely think of the difficulties encountered when warning others to flee a burning building or seek shelter in a storm. Why should sharing the gospel be any different?

The gospel message has life-transforming power. When you, and other members of your church, begin sharing this message, it makes a phenomenal impact, explainable only in terms of God! This is the ministry of your church, a ministry that leaves the world with nothing of similar comparison, a ministry that often overwhelms any criticism and shuts the mouth of the skeptic.

Jesus makes somebodies out of nobodies.

Jesus makes somebodies out of nobodies. That's what the Sanhedrin concluded as they sized up Peter and John. Read Acts 4:13. Peter and John were considered _____ and _____ men! As rough fishermen from up north, they were unaccustomed to city ways, not to mention a trial by the religious big shots of their day. Yet they had seized control of the trial, and now it was their accusers who were in a panic. Where did this boldness come from? In the words of the Sanhedrin, *"They had been with Jesus."*

82

What does *"They had been with Jesus"* mean to you?

_____

_____

Once, while visiting on a college campus where I served as trustee, I was approached by a bright-eyed coed. "Brother Tom, do you remember me?" she asked. Looking into her face, a flood of memories almost overwhelmed me. Yes. I remembered when our bus ministers found her in an abusive home with alcoholic parents. I remembered her mischievousness at church and later at camp. I remembered when she had trusted Christ and then followed Him in baptism. But I was unprepared for what came next. "Brother Tom," she said, "I am about to graduate at the top of my class!" Here was a young girl destined to become a nobody, who through Christ, had become a somebody.

What parts of the body of Christ would have had an impact on this young woman's life?

❑ those who were teachers
❑ those who drove the bus
❑ those who gave money to provide curriculum, Bibles, a place to meet
❑ those who prayed
❑ all who loved her
❑ other _____

We can all be part of leading someone to Christ.

Thank God for your church and the life-changing message and ministry it shares with your community and around the world.

Day Four
Compelled to Tell Others

" 'Whether it's right in the sight of God [for us] to listen to you rather than to God, you decide; for we are unable to stop speaking about what we have seen and heard' " (Acts 4:19-20).

As a member of a local church, Kingdom Family members are

inspired to participate in a unique combination of ministry and missions. It is more than a matter of obeying Christ's command to " *'make disciples of all nations' " (Matt. 28:19)*. They operate from an inner compulsion that springs out of their own personal experience with Christ. They cannot help but share the good news because it means so much to them.

This was what the council discovered in Peter and John. Their inspiration did not spring from selfish purposes. It was from the work of God's Spirit in their lives! Let's return to the scene in the temple. The religious leaders are discussing what their next step should be.

Read Acts 4:14-18 and answer the following questions. What complicated the issue for the Sanhedrin, making it difficult for them to deal with Peter and John?

_____

Who else besides them had seen this healing miracle?

_____

Peter and John could not stop speaking what they had seen and heard

What was their solution?
❏ just forget it ❏ put Peter and John back in prison
❏ ordered Peter and John not to preach in Jesus' name

Now read Acts 4:19-20. Peter's concern was listening to _____ rather than _____.

What did Peter say that he and John must do because of what they had seen and heard?

_____

Their actions were inspired by both the command of the Lord (*"what we have seen and heard"*) and the inner compulsion of God's Spirit (*"we are unable to stop speaking"*).

Think about what you have read in the four Gospels: Matthew, Mark, Luke, and John. Name three specific things that the disciples had seen and heard:

1. _____

2. _____

3. _____

What have

you seen

and heard?

Now list in the margin some evidences of Christ's transforming power that you have witnessed.

The last verse that John wrote alluded that they saw more than what was written down. *"Jesus did many other things as well. If every one of them were written down, I suppose that even the whole world would not have room for the books that would be written"* (John 21:25).

For many years I have sent prayer letters to church members. I tell them that on a specific date in the future I will be praying for them by name, and I ask them to provide me with a list of their prayer concerns. Reading those letters has become an incredible blessing to me. It has helped me get to know my flock in ways far deeper than I could ever know them through casual conversation.

I referred to one of these letters on page 86. In other words, like Peter and John, this young woman can't help but speak and teach the things she had seen of Christ. That's the inspiration for the church's mission … your mission.

Day Five
On a Mission with Limited Time

"Let us be concerned about one another in order to promote love and good works, not staying away from our meetings, as some habitually do, but encouraging each other, and all the more as you see the day drawing near" (Heb. 10:24-25).

Let's visit the temple courtyard one last time. Standing before the Sanhedrin, Peter and John could recall the incredible moment that had transpired only a few days earlier as they were gathered with Christ on a nearby hillside. That moment set the stage for their ministry and defined the urgency of the hour. Jesus had spoken to them, assuring them that the Holy Spirit would come and help them fulfill His commission (Acts 1:8).

Now read Acts 1:9-11. What had happened to Jesus after He finished speaking?
❏ He walked away   ❏ He ascended into heaven.

What question did the angels ask His followers?

_____

Just like Jesus' followers, we look into heaven, awaiting His return. Jesus, Himself promised that He would return. (Read John 14:1-3.)

According to 1 Thessalonians 5:2, how did Paul describe Jesus' return in his letter to the Thessalonians?

_____

We don't plan for a thief to come to our house, but we should be prepared if one does. Paul uses two words in 1 Thessalonians 5:6 to describe the way we are to live. We are to
_____ and _____.

How do you prepare against a thief's attack?

How can you *stay awake* and *be sober*?

_____

We eagerly anticipate that moment when Jesus calls the church unto Himself. And we know that, in the meantime, we are to heed the example of Christ, who said, " '*I must do the works of Him who sent Me while it is day. Night is coming when no one can work*' " (John 9:4). Like Christ, we are on a mission, and our time is limited.

We find Jesus' mission in Luke 4:18-19. Read these verses and check the ministries Christ came to fulfill.

- ❑ preach good news to the poor
- ❑ proclaim freedom to the captives
- ❑ recovery of sight to the blind
- ❑ set free the oppressed
- ❑ proclaim the year of the Lord's favor

Are we to join Christ in this ministry? Yes! Jesus said His ministry is to be ours as well.

The writer of Hebrews challenges us to continue meeting together so that we can encourage one another to promote love and good works (Heb 10:24-25). How can you encourage someone today?

_____

_____

Let's continue meeting together to encourage one another.

Christ said that He would build His church! He invites you to join Him in this awesome mission. What are you waiting for? Right now is the time to commit to sharing the good news energetically and faithfully. Even as you pray, God may be setting things in motion for His Son to call home His Bride. Ready? Set? Let's go!

WEEK SIX

Using Time Wisely and Practicing Biblical Stewardship

"Trust in the LORD with all your heart, and do not rely on your own understanding; think about Him in all your ways, and He will guide you on the right paths" (Prov. 3:5-6).

Once, after spending a period of meditation on Ephesians 5:17, I had a dream the following night. In my dream I was standing on the side of a mountain, looking down on a valley below. In that valley I saw a huge multitude of unusual animals of many shapes and sizes. The animals were representations of my time! Huge, elephants represented years, smaller cattle represented months, and even smaller creatures representing weeks and days; birds and insects represented minutes and seconds.

I noticed that they all were moving in the same direction. Toward the far end of the valley, I saw someone standing by an open gate. Whoever was by that gate was allowing these animals (my time) to get out without my permission! I hurried down to stop him.

"Who are you?" I asked.
"Why," he said, "I'm the devil!"
"What are you doing with all my time?" I urged.
"I'm a time rustler, and I've got good use for all this time," he said.
"Well, you can't have it!" I protested.
"Why not?" he asked. "After all, you don't have any plans for it!"

Day One
No Regret, No Remorse, No Return

"Don't be foolish, but understand what the Lord's will is" (Eph. 5:17).

Pillars five and six share one important characteristic. They both call for the exercise of stewardship. We will look at both of these pillars this week. Don't worry! You won't have twice the work.

The popularity of time management and ordering your priorities indicates the struggle we experience when we seek to be good stewards of our time. Many of us have signed up for seminars, purchased books, video or audio CDs, in an attempt to find the secrets that will set us free from the time trap. The good news is that such secrets exist and are available to anyone willing to hear. They are found in God's timeless book, the Bible.

List the various things you have done in an attempt to make the best use of your time.

_____

_____

How effective have these efforts been? How costly? Were they worth the effort and cost?

_____

_____

Often we are looking for a quick solution to an age-old problem.

Don't get me wrong. The fact that you care about your use of time speaks volumes about your character. But often we are looking for a quick solution to an age-old problem. Time, like everything else God has created, is a limited, non-renewable resource that has been entrusted to us. Because of this, we must know what is involved in the proper stewardship of it. After all, each of us will one day give an account to God for how we have spent our time.

Because time is God's creation we must each account to Him for how we use it. Paul reminds us in Ephesians 5:16 that *"we are to _____ the time because the days are evil."*

The story on this week's opening page reflects this Scripture. Instead of speaking with my Heavenly Father, though, I dreamed I was conversing with the devil himself. He reminded me that since I had not made plans for my time, he would be more than happy to do so. Ouch!

Reflect over what you did the past 24 hours. Estimate how much time you spent:

How have you spent your time?

Sleeping _____

Eating _____

Working _____

Exercising _____

Reading a helpful book _____

Being on the computer _____

Watching television _____

In personal Bible Study and prayer _____

With your family _____

In worship or witnessing _____

Just doing nothing in particular _____

Did you use all of your time wisely? Will God have been honored by how you spent your time?

Some people have a remarkable capacity for living life to the fullest and leaving a legacy that lasts far beyond their years. Others seem to quit living before their lives come to an end. Unfortunately, the impact of their lives is scarcely felt beyond their funeral.

I recall that my paternal grandfather preached his last sermon just two days before his death at age 92. My maternal grandfather farmed until the age of 95. That year he actually considered planting seedlings for a future timber harvest!

Remembering the experience of my two grandfathers, I must realize that it's possible I may have as many years of active life ahead of me as behind. On the other hand, God may have an entirely different plan. He may know that I should be thinking about years or months of service rather than decades.

Who lives life to the fullest?

Who do you know that fits the first category of people? (They lived life to the fullest.) Write their name in the margin.

Who fits the second category? (Quitting before their life came to an end.) Write their name in the margin.

Who quits before their life is over?

Time, like everything else in God's created order, fell under the curse of sin when Adam and Eve rebelled against Him in the garden of Eden. Like everything else, it must be redeemed if it is to bring glory to God and benefit to man. You must take deliberate steps to use time wisely. Your adversary already has plans for your time, and you must actively redeem or rescue it from him. That is why the apostle Paul exhorts us to walk wisely, *"redeeming the time, because the days are evil"* (Eph. 5:16, KJV).

The word translated *redeem* means "to rescue from loss, or to buy back." If you had a chance to buy back some hours from yesterday, what would you do differently?

_____

_____

The only way to use time wisely is to understand what God's will is and walk in it.

To redeem time, God doesn't want us to be foolish, but *"to understand what the will of the Lord is"* (Eph. 5:16, KJV). This means that the only way to use time wisely is to understand what God's will is and walk in it.

Proverbs 3:5-6 tells us how we can have God-directed paths. Fill in the blanks to finish the verses.
"_____ in the LORD with _____ your heart, and do not rely on your _____ understanding; think about Him in _____ your ways, and He _____ guide you on the right paths."

Finish today's study by reading the story of one who trusted the Lord with all of his heart and left the results to God.

William Borden, one of Yale's most enterprising students of the last century, turned his back on a lucrative career in business. Instead he headed to Egypt to join a team of missionaries, and was stricken with a disease that would quickly claim his life.

Friends, who doubted his call, wrote letters urging him to return home. His reply was simple, "No regret, no remorse, no return." Was he a poor steward of his brief life? You decide. Literally thousands of people have been stirred to mission service by his example of sacrifice and devotion.

Day Two
Seek the Lord

"In Your behalf my heart says, 'Seek My face.' LORD, I will seek Your face" (Ps. 27:8).

Yesterday we learned that using our time wisely requires that we depart from our own assumptions and operate from the basis of God's point of view, rather than our own. We will *lean not on [our] own understanding.* We will reject any counsel that encourages us to violate the clear principles of God as revealed in the Scripture, choosing instead to utilize our time in a way that pleases our Lord.

The prophet Daniel's personal use of time was significantly different from the norms of the society in which he lived. Daniel made it a habit to pray to God three times a day. Several governmental officials decided to set him up. Read about this in Daniel 6:7-9.

What did the officials ask the king to do?

_____

What would be the penalty for breaking this decree?

_____

The moment the decree was signed forbidding prayer to anyone other than Darius, Daniel went to his home and prayed as he had always done. Daniel 6:10 tells us that the decree didn't affect how Daniel spent his time. Daniel would not obey a decree that charged him to disobey his God.

Perhaps you remember the story. Daniel was caught and thrown into the lion's den. After sweating it out through the night, King Darius hurried to the lion's den at *very early in the morning* (v. 19).

Now read Daniel 6:20-28. What had happened to Daniel in the den of lions? _____

You probably won't face hungry lions, but what comparison can you make? Recall a time in your life when you chose to trust God and had to pay a high price.

Recall the story here.

_____

_____

Using our time wisely demands a certain level of discipline. Our conduct will be guided by the lordship of Christ over our lives and

After hearing the decree, Daniel went home and prayed as he had always done.

our desire to enter into fellowship with Him. We will seek to acknowledge Him in all our ways. Our use of time will be principled on the one hand yet dynamically guided by our disciplined looking to Him on the other.

When reading the Psalms, we see this practice in action. David repeatedly speaks of seeking God's face. Read several of these passages where David cries out to God. Write the common word you find in each verse.

In Your behalf my heart says, "_____ My face." LORD, I will _____ Your face (Ps. 27:8).

Happy are those who keep His decrees and _____ Him with all their heart (Ps. 119:2).

God used David significantly as he took time every day to seek God's face. David sought God's direction to turn or to stay and acted in concert with His will. Now read about others who disciplined themselves to seek God faithfully every day.

Martin Luther spoke of having so much to do that he could not think of beginning each day without spending at least four hours in prayer.

Who has made a significant impact on others?

Hudson Taylor, mission pioneer and founder of the China Inland Mission (now called the Overseas Missionary Fellowship), spent grueling days in travel. Yet those travelling with him wrote of seeing the flicker of a candle behind his curtain around two o'clock each morning and knowing he was having his time with God.

David Brainerd's diary tells of nights of prayer in spite of a debilitating illness that took his life at the age of thirty. No wonder it is said that God brought revival among the Native Americans along the eastern seaboard on the wings of Brainerd's prayers.

Whom do you know whose daily time with the Lord has made a significant impact on others? Write that person's name in the margin.

What impact has been felt because of this person's faithfulness?

_____

_____

God has promised that we can have His direction for our paths. In other words, we can redeem the time, using it for our benefit and His glory. It is a matter of acknowledging Him *in all our ways,* whether the seemingly insignificant or the obviously important.

Sometimes we think that the things done to God's glory must be big, significant, and attention grabbing. In reality, God is not so much honored by our doing great things as He is in our doing all the things He puts before us in a great way.

As we order our lives in concert with God's will, we have sufficient time for personal growth through prayer, for the study of God's Word, and for fulfilling every God-given responsibility related to our family.

God has incredible blessings in store for those who are committed to using their time wisely. One day you will give an account to Him for how you have spent this nonrenewable resource entrusted to your care. Pause to thank God for the gift of time. Ask Him to help you use it wisely.

God has blessings for those committed to using their time wisely.

Day Three
A Spirit of Reverence

"The earth and everything in it … belong to the Lord; for He laid its foundation" (Ps. 24:1-2).

Today we turn our attention to exercising biblical stewardship. Good stewardship is the result of a commitment to specific biblical principles. By following these principles, many members of God's Kingdom family are touching the lives of others for the kingdom's sake and giving faithful support to their local church. Good stewardship is a practice that makes life an exhilarating adventure of earthly impact and eternal significance.

Today and tomorrow, you will be examining specific principles that will help you exercise wise and biblical stewardship over your resources. For your benefit I have placed these principles into three main groups: The Principles of Reverence, The Principles of Responsibility, and The Principles of Restoration. Note that several "principles" appear under each heading. As you read through each principle, stop, reflect, and let God speak to your heart, then agree with Him before moving to the next principle.

Stewardship must be approached with a spirit of reverence.

The Principles of Reverence
Stewardship must be approached with a spirit of reverence. It is, at its heart, a matter of relationship. In other words, the way we handle the resources entrusted to us speaks volumes about our respect for the One who has assigned them to our care.

Principle 1: God owns everything; we own nothing.
Your house, possessions, family, time, abilities, even your own body belong to God and should be treated as such. Read the following verses and answer the questions.

Psalm 24:1-2: Why does the earth belong to God? _____

Psalm 50:12: How much of this world is God's? _____

Col. 1:16: For whom was our world created? _____

As a young boy, my next-door neighbor felt that all boys my age should grow up with a love for baseball. We spent endless hours playing catch, looking over baseball cards, listening to games on the radio, and actually going to a few games when time and money afforded. He ate, slept, and lived the game. One afternoon our baseball finally fell apart. We had taped up the torn stitches and scuffed rawhide, but its use had come to an end. I didn't have another one, and neither did he. Well, almost. My friend went inside, returning a few minutes later with a perfectly good baseball, now browned with age.

"I guess we can use this," he said. "It's a home run ball hit by Mickey Mantle over the center-field fence. I caught it on the second bounce in the bleachers."

I was almost afraid to touch the ball, much less throw it! To me it was more valuable than silver or gold. The last thing I wanted to do was throw an errant pitch that would land the ball in the street or against the fence. And Micky Mantle's fingerprints weren't even on the ball.

What you have was entrusted to you by the God of the universe, the One who made you along with everything else in all of creation, the One who has provided for your salvation, the One to whom you must give an ultimate account. His fingerprints are on everything...including you.

Are you showing reverence for Him by the manner in which you oversee what He has entrusted to your care? ❑ yes ❑ no

Principle 2: God has designated us as stewards of what belongs to Him.

A steward does not own; he oversees, or manages, what is owned by another. A steward must use what has been entrusted to him in a manner that honors his master, his master's desires, and his master's ownership.

Jesus told a parable of the wise manager. Read this story in Luke 12:42-48. The summary of this parable is found in the latter part of verse 48. Write it in the margin.

God gave you the position of stewardship. You have a choice regarding how you perform your responsibility. Have you ever taken time to thank God for the privilege of being a steward over that which belongs to Him? Take time now to thank God for this responsibility. Ask Him to guide you to be a responsible steward.

We are to be stewards of what belongs to God.

If we are responsible stewards, God will provide for our needs.

Principle 3: When we act responsibly as overseers, God provides for every need.

Nothing delights the heart of a master so much as a steward who acts responsibly. Faithfulness to the master's best interest is the single most important requirement of a steward. In fact, Scripture reminds us that *"it is required in stewards, that a man be found faithful"* (1 Cor. 4:2, KJV). God promises that those who are faithful in their stewardship over His creation will have every need met and every godly desire satisfied.

You will find this promise in two verses of Scripture listed below. Fill in the missing word in both verses.

Seek first the kingdom of God and His righteousness, and _____ these things will be provided for you (Matt. 6:33).

My God will supply _____ your needs according to His riches in glory in Christ Jesus (Phil. 4:19).

Are you confident that God is not only capable but also willing to meet all of your needs and fulfill every godly desire of your heart?

We will give an account for our steward-ship.

Principle 4: We will each give an account for our stewardship.

How have you used what has been entrusted to your care? A judgment will happen that will take into account all you have been given: material resources, physical bodies, opportunities, abilities, spiritual giftedness, and time. This is called the Judgment Seat of Christ. It is for believers. At stake will not be whether you will enter heaven. Instead, the Lord will ask, "What did you do with what you were given?"

Jesus intimates that this Judgment becomes the basis for rewards in heaven. Read more about this in Matthew 25:14-30. Rate yourself as a steward.

0	5	10
lousy, unwise careless	indifferent and wise	very good

Rate how God might look at your stewardship.

```
|    |    |    |    |    |    |    |    |    |    |
0                        5                        10
lousy, unwise            indifferent              very good
careless                 and wise
```

Did you have different answers? If so, pause now to ask God to help you become a wise steward. As you do, He *"will supply all your needs according to His riches in glory in Christ Jesus"* (Phil. 4:19).

Day Four
Responsibilities of Stewardship

"Whether you eat or drink, or whatever you do, do everything for God's glory" (1 Cor. 10:31).

We've learned that as members of God's Kingdom Family, we must give an account for what we have done with what we have been given. But what does our Master expects of us? His standards are clearly spelled out for us in Scripture. These are the Principles of Responsibility, and they describe how we are to perform our stewardship.

Principles of Responsibility
Principle 1: As stewards, our primary responsibility is to glorify God.

In Jesus' parable of the large banquet (Luke 14:16-24), the one concern of the servant was to fulfill the master's desire. How he must have grieved to report, *" 'What you have ordered has been done, and there's still room' "* (v. 12). The servant wanted to honor his master's wishes for a banquet hall filled with guests.

Read this parable. Check any of the following excuses people gave for not attending the banquet.
- ❑ bought a field and had to see it
- ❑ bought oxen and had to try them out
- ❑ just got married
- ❑ wasn't interested

What is our primary responsibility as God's steward?

99

Because of the servant's report of these excuses, the master told him to find others to attend. In fact the slave was ordered out still another time so that the banquet hall would be filled. How did the servant respond to the commands of his master?

_____

_____

Whose honor was of concern to the servant? _____

We are not accountable for what God has not entrusted to our care.

Principle 2: We are to be good stewards of our home, church, state, body, soul, and spirit.
The Lord does not hold us accountable for what He has not entrusted to our care. Let's look briefly at six areas in which we are given specific stewardship responsibilities.

Stewardship at Home
God expects members of His Kingdom Family to take care of things at home. Husbands and fathers are reminded that "*if anyone does not provide for his own relatives, and especially for his household, he has denied the faith and is worse than an unbeliever*" (1 Tim. 5:8). Wives and mothers are challenged by the example of the virtuous woman who "*watches over the activities of her household*" (Prov. 31:27).

Your home is the laboratory where the principles of God are put to the test, proven true, and modeled for the generations to come.

Stewardship in the Church
God's plan is for the ministry of the church to move forward with tithes, offerings, and sacrificial giving brought by each member. As New Testament believers, our commitment should at least exceed those who lived under the law rather than grace. They were to "*bring all the tithes [the first, or set-aside tenth] into the storehouse*" (Mal. 3:10, NKJV). Paul's commendation to the churches in Galatia are instructive. They brought their offerings "*on the first day of the week*" (1 Cor. 16:2).

We read and understand that we are to give. But in what manner should we give? Check any of the following that apply.

❏ cheerfully   ❏ grudgingly
❏ as a privilege   ❏ because it is a duty

These same people found giving to be a joyful privilege because *"they gave themselves especially to the Lord"* (2 Cor. 8:5). Once you have settled that Jesus is Lord of all, giving to the church becomes a matter of simple and joyous submission to His will.

Stewardship within the State

Being members of God's Kingdom Family does not exempt us from responsibilities to our government. Paul exhorts us to *"submit to the governing authority, for there is no authority except from God, and those that exist are instituted by God"* (Rom. 13:1). Then he echoes Christ's words: *"Pay your obligations to everyone: taxes to those you owe taxes, tolls to those you owe tolls, respect to those you owe respect, and honor to those you owe honor"* (Rom. 13:7).

Pay your obligations to everyone.

From the Scripture passages above, should a Christian be diligent and honest in paying the taxes levied by government? ❏ yes   ❏ no

Stewardship of the Body

We also must consider the importance of stewardship over our physical bodies. God has entrusted to you a physical body and it should be used for His glory. It is, after all, *"a sanctuary of the Holy Spirit,"* and you are exhorted to *"glorify God in your body"* (1 Cor. 6:19-20).

Some people have no balance in this area, either totally ignoring the importance of physical well-being or spending hours in the gym to the detriment of their family, church, or other responsibilities. A friend involved in physical fitness once told me that one of the reasons he stayed so fit was so that he could be on earth longer to tell more people about Jesus.

When was the last time you took a walk for exercise? _____

Plan to take a walk this week. If the weather will not permit a walk outside, find a place indoors to walk. Think about the responsibility you have to take care of your physical body.

Stewardship of the Soul
Your soul (intellect, will, and emotions) is given to you as a sacred trust, and it is to be used with the utmost care.

"Garbage In, Garbage Out" still applies.

The old computer analogy still applies: Garbage in, garbage out. Read Matthew 12:33-37 to know the context in which Jesus talks about the heart.

If you are building a storeroom of good, what will the results be?

_____

If you are building a storeroom of evil, what will be produced?

_____

Stewardship of the Spirit
Again Paul's reminder to the Corinthian believers is worth noting: *"Glorify God in your body* and in your spirit (emphasis mine) *which are God's"* (1 Cor. 6:20).

Rather than giving place to those things that hinder communion with our Master, our worship and praise of Him, we should commit to those things that will make us strong in spirit.

Read Ephesians 6:10. What is our only hope of success when engaged in spiritual warfare?

_____

Principle 3: God has designated specific methods by which we can successfully fulfill our stewardship responsibilities.
God never asks us to assume a responsibility without providing the means by which we may succeed. The following six methods

are biblical, proven, and effective in times of financial crisis as well as prosperity.

This next exercise will help to summarize the methods and their biblical basis. On the left, you will find the six methods. On the right, you will find one or two Scriptures as reference to the methods listed. Match the method with the Scripture.

___ A righteous life   a. Matthew 10:16
___ A devotional life   b. Proverbs 22:4; Matthew 6:33
___ A diligent life   c. Malachi 3:10; Luke 6:38
___ A giving life   d. John 15:7
___ A disciplined life   e. Proverbs 12:11; Proverbs 13:4
___ A discerning life   f. Philippians 4:11-12; 1 Timothy 6:6

Good stewards reflect these characteristics. Do the six methods above seem like too much to expect? ❏ yes ❏ no

If you are struggling in an area of stewardship, confess it to the Lord, accept His forgiveness, ask for His grace and determine to honor Him by your obedience.

Day Five
Find Restoration

"The God of all grace, who called you to His eternal glory in Christ Jesus, will personally restore, establish, strengthen, and support you after you have suffered a little" (1 Pet. 5:10).

Perhaps as you have examined God's principles for exercising wise stewardship you have become aware that you are violating some of them. How can you experience restoration?

The Principles of Restoration
Principle 1: Restoration always begins with repentance.
Before reading the explanations below, in the margin write your own definition of confession and repentance.

Restoration always begins with repentance.

Let's see what God's Word says about confession and repentance. Confessing our sin means that we agree with God that we have sinned in specific ways. The word translated *confess* means "to say the same thing."

Read 1 John 1:9. If we confess our sins, what will God do?

_____

Repentance, on the other hand, means to do an about-face, turning away from sin and toward God. The word translated "confess" refers to a change of mind that results in a change of action. It is an *action*, not simply an *attitude*.

In reality, you have not repented of a sin you are still _____.

If you are still practicing poor stewardship, you may have confessed to that reality but you have yet to repent. Repentance is critical and essential for restoration. *"The one who conceals his sins will not prosper [or make progress]"* (Prov. 28:13).

If you have not taken time to confess sins of poor stewardship, do so now. Be specific. Ask God for grace to repent, to change your behavior. Cooperate with Him by obeying His Word.

Principle 2: Tithing and giving must become a way of life.
Through tithing and giving you invite God into your finances.

Tithing and giving must become a way of life.

A friend candidly admitted to me that he struggled with both the precept and the practice of tithing. He said, "To be honest, I simply do not make enough money to go around. I have bills to pay, food and clothing for my family, and all the usual expenses. Unexpected situations always seem to rise. Nothing is left after all these expenses, so how can I tithe?"

I explained to my friend that the tithe should be his first concern. The word translated *tithe* means "the first, or set aside tenth." I explained that tithing is an act of faith that invites the Lord's blessing on our resources. Some time later he approached me with a sheepish smile. He explained that for several months he had been practicing the principle of tithing. "It's amazing!" he exclaimed. "All the bills are paid, and we actually have been able to place money in savings for the first time in our married life!" My friend was experiencing the restoration that comes from repentance! Now he was ready to learn about giving…the practice of supplying for others *above and beyond* the tithe that already is the Lord's.

Read Malachi 3:10-12. What does God call someone who ignores the practice of tithing and giving?

_____

As God looks at your practice of tithing and giving, what must He call you?

_____

Principle 3: Eliminating nonessentials shortens the journey.
Many people are saddened by their financial situation but unwilling to eliminate the practices that got them there. One of those practices is the accumulation of things that might be called nonessential. These things are enjoyable, but unnecessary. In reality, it is theft to retain something while overdue in your payments to a creditor simply because you enjoy owning and using it.

What do you own?

List in the margin several items you own. Mark a line through those you consider to be non-essential.

Eliminating nonessentials can be an exciting exercise, bringing a new discipline to your life as well as a new sense of contentment.

Read 1 Timothy 6:6. What did Paul say is the result of godliness with contentment?

_____

Let creditors know you care.

Principle 4: Your creditors need to know you care.
No one likes to face people to whom they are in debt. But if you have made poor financial choices, approach your creditors before they approach you. Work out a manageable payment system as quickly as possible. The sacrifice will be worth the pain to eliminate the burden.

According to Proverbs 20:18, how important is wise counsel?

_____

If you are in this situation, whom can you call for help?_____

Be patient!

Principle 5: Restoration requires patience.
Recovering from the distress caused by poor stewardship often takes time and patience. Patiently pursuing God's plan will lead to complete restoration, recovery, and a renewed appreciation for your responsibility.

Be encouraged with the words James wrote us in his letter: *"Consider it a great joy, my brothers, whenever you experience various trials, knowing that the testing of your faith produces endurance. But endurance must do its complete work, so that you may be mature and complete, lacking nothing"* (Jas. 1:2-4).

Underline the words in the verses above that encourage you.

God has a way out of the distress caused by unwise and unfaithful stewardship. Every Christian should make an honest effort to be free from the kind of financial burdens that strangle usefulness, destroy effectiveness, and rob us of joy.

End today's study by reflecting on a promise God made through His servant Paul: *"God is able to make every grace overflow to you, so that in every way, always having everything you need, you may excel in every good work"* (2 Cor. 9:8).

106

Sharing the Gospel of Jesus Christ

" 'Go, therefore, and make disciples of all nations, baptizing them in the name of the Father and of the Son and of the Holy Spirit, teaching them to observe everything I have commanded you. And remember, I am with you always, to the end of the age' " (Matt. 28:19-20).

Bob and Peggy Oxford live in Denver, Colorado, where they are members of the Applewood Baptist Church. Bob is a petroleum engineer, a businessman, and founder of a nationwide consulting firm. For the past few years Peggy has worked beside him in this family owned and operated business. But their life is consumed with a passion to use everything God has provided to share the gospel and encourage others to do the same.

Several times a year the Oxfords have participated together in short-term overseas mission projects where they have been joined by their children and most recently their grandchildren. But their favorite responsibilities relate to the mission endeavors of their church. Their home has been opened to countless visitors, both nationals and foreigners, who have found a warm-hearted welcome and an eagerness to talk about Jesus.

International students and business people are their favorite guests. The Oxfords keep up with them, visit and correspond with them, even though the list grows each month. During the fifty years of their married life, the Oxfords have sought to be careful stewards of the resources entrusted to them, determined to make them count for Christ's sake and the kingdom's.

Day One
A Passion to Fulfill the Great Commission

"I am not ashamed of the gospel, because it is God's power for salvation to everyone who believes, first to the Jew, and also to the Greek" (Rom. 1:16).

Who do you know needs to hear and respond to the gospel?

Perhaps the most unique attribute members of God's Kingdom Family have is their consistent eagerness to share the gospel with others. "Others" may include their family, neighbors, work or school associates, and people around the world.

Name six people you believe need to hear and respond to the gospel. Write their names in the margin.

Even if Kingdom Family members are the only believers in their home or workplace, their personal experience with Christ changes the atmosphere where they live and work. Christ, living in them, begins to reach out to others through them.

Who reached out to you to share Christ's love? _____

Who have you reached out to? _____

Let me share this story of a friend. Originally alone in his family as a believer, he has been joined by his wife, then his two children and his mother. He took a second job doing night deliveries for a local pizza chain to help relieve financial strain. The Holy Spirit prompted him to add the story of his personal conversion to Christ. Once the delivery was made and payment was received, he asked, "Could I leave with you the story of my life?" Upon receiving an affirmative reply, he would hand them his typed story.

Imagine our surprise when we received a call at church from someone wanting to know how they could find what their pizza deliveryman called his "new life." Later we discovered that he had placed our church's phone number at the bottom of the page!

Read today's Scripture verse. Paul said that he wasn't ashamed of the gospel. In fact, he was eager to share the good news, even in Rome. What did he say was so special about this news?

_____

Our Lord's final instructions before ascending to heaven was a clear reminder that they were to be His witnesses, beginning in Jerusalem and spreading ultimately to the ends of the earth.

Read Acts 1:8 and answer the following questions.

1. How are Christ's followers to be empowered for witnessing?

_____

2. What are Christ's followers to be? _____

3. What limits did Christ put on this commission? _____

Recently I called the home of a church member to share some information with her husband. "Pastor," the man's wife said almost in a whisper, "I apologize, but I'm in the middle of a Bible study with women from my neighborhood. Do you know about my Bible study?" I confessed my surprise. Like others, they were using their home to model missions involvement for their children.

In our church, new members are urged to get and maintain a current passport. We believe that few things can so expand the vision of a believer as personal participation in overseas missions.

Have you participated in a mission project? (It doesn't have to be overseas.) If so, tell where and when.

_____

_____

We are to be God's witnesses to the world.

If you have children, how are you modeling participation in the Great Commission to them?

_____

Mission projects can help the concept of a sacrificial lifestyle become a reality. These projects should be significant enough that lifestyle changes must take place for them to be completed successfully. After all, if you can still live, wear, go, spend, drive, and eat in the same manner as before, then nothing has been sacrificed. Sacrifice requires an alteration in our lifestyle; something is given up for God's higher cause.

Jesus said we need to sacrifice to follow Him.

Jesus spoke of the necessity for sacrifice if we are to follow Him. We read this in Matthew 16:24. " *'If anyone wants to come with Me, he must deny himself, take up his cross and follow Me.'* "

What does Jesus mean by *"deny himself?"* _____

What does He mean by *"take up his cross?"* _____

A growing number of families are seeing the value of a family mission trip. This helps them plan and pray together as they anticipate their days on the field. Together they begin to set aside resources for the trip, praying that the Lord will bless their days.

If you could plan a family mission trip, where would you go?

_____

What would each family member do? _____

_____

What are you willing to sacrifice to make such a trip possible?

_____

Underlying all that a Kingdom Family does regarding missions is the growing assumption that every family member will participate in fulfilling the Great Commission. They even face the possibility of God's call to a lifetime of missions with joyful eagerness.

Close today's study by asking God to help you see your world through His eyes.

Day Two
Compelling Realities

"Rescue those being taken off to death" (Prov. 24:11).

What is the driving force behind the Kingdom Family movement? Members of God's Kingdom Family have a firm grasp on four heart-stirring issues. These issues are spelled out clearly in Proverbs 24:10-12.

If you do nothing in a difficult time,
your strength is limited.
Rescue those being taken off to death,
and save those stumbling toward slaughter.
If you say, "But we didn't know about this,"
won't He who weighs hearts consider it?
Won't He who protects your life know?
Won't He repay a person according to his work?

Write in the margin your thoughts about this passage.

Three phrases will help you understand the plight of people without Christ. Let's study them together.

1. People without Christ are helplessly lost. They are *"being taken off to death"* (Prov. 24:11). Picture a blind man being taken by the hand. He believes he is being led to safety and life. But no! The Adversary is leading him to death.

Ask God to help you see your world through His eyes.

111

Who does God want to use to rescue this man? _____

How important is it for him to be rescued now?

_____

What title would you give this photograph?

2. People without Christ are hopelessly lost. They are *"stumbling toward slaughter"* (Prov. 24:11). The picture here is of a person who has started tumbling down the side of a steep, rocky hill. They cannot gain footing as the loose rock gives way beneath them. What's more, they see nothing to reach for to stop their fall.

Years ago I sat riveted by a photograph in a local newspaper. A man was being swept downstream to certain death. On the shore, another was reaching out with a stick, urging the man to grab hold. But you could see from the distance between them and the look of panic on the victim's face that it was too little, too late. In seconds he would be drowned.

A person who rejects Christ has given up his only hope for salvation. Read Hebrews 10:26-29. Write down the three things a person who rejects Christ has done. (See v. 29.)

1. _____

2. _____

3. _____

Without Christ a person is hopelessly lost! Who has the responsibility of sharing Christ with this person? _____

3. People without Christ are hellishly lost. They are *"being taken off to death"* (Prov. 24:11), an eternity separated from God in a place called hell.

Read the Lord's account of two deaths in Luke 16:19-31. Jesus gives a graphic account of what happens when people die in unbelief. Beside each statement write the verse from this passage that supports it.

The rich man was in an actual place _____

The rich man was in an awful place _____

The rich man was in an alone place _____

The rich man was in an always place _____

The rich man was in an acceptable place _____

The rich man was in an avoidable place _____

Who has the responsibility for warning unbelievers about their eternal destiny? _____

William Booth, founder of the Salvation Army, stated that the best training for any witness would be to spend five minutes in hell. As you complete today's study, ask God to show you the terrible plight of the unsaved. Remember that this group includes every unbeliever, even those among your family and friends. Let that thought compel you to action.

Day Three
Critical Responsibilities

"Rescue those being taken off to death, and save those stumbling toward slaughter" (Prov. 24:11).

Members of God's Kingdom Family are aware that in light of the compelling realities that we studied yesterday, they must accept the critical responsibilities God has assigned to them ... and they must do it without delay!

Some years ago one of the fiercest tornadoes in America's history

The best training for a Christian would be to spend five minutes in hell.

swept through our town, only narrowly missing our church. I had gathered in the church building with my family, neighboring families, and other church members to escape the pending storm. Once the winds died down, we came out to survey the devastation. Knowing many people, including some of our own, were trapped in the rubble, we immediately began a search-and-rescue effort.

I will never forget that night! We ran, stumbling over the debris, shouting, "Is anyone in there? Does anyone need help?" Later, as some of us were trying to get strength for a second effort, I looked at our little band of rescuers. No one had given a thought to what they were wearing or what the effort would do to our clothing. We were desperate because we knew lives were at stake.

We knew lives were at stake.

Two commands are found in our focal passage that every Kingdom Family member must obey. Look at the passage carefully. Write these two commands.

1. _____

2. _____

We are to *"rescue those being taken off to death"* (Prov. 24:11). In other words, we cannot allow them to die without our intervention. At some point they must hear the gospel and have an opportunity to respond.

What are some things you and your family might do to open up an opportunity to share the gospel with an acquaintance?

_____

Have you heard of "negligent homicide?" This term describes the act of allowing someone to die by neglect. Recently our news was filled with the sad story of a woman who neglected her young baby, leaving her in a car while she stopped by for a drink at the local bar. Bystanders later saw the child and sought to rescue her. It was too late! The child's body temperature had soared in the suffocating heat of the automobile. The mother was arrested on charges on negligent homicide.

What term would you use to describe a Christian who neglected to tell an unsaved neighbor about Christ?

_____

2. We are to *"save those stumbling toward slaughter"* (Prov. 24:11). Living in your neighborhood, working beside you at the office or plant, attending your same school, playing on your team, is no guarantee that a person will receive Christ. But it should give them some advantage! You should be doing what you can to hold them back from their unbelief and its horrible consequences.

Read Ezekiel 3:16-21. A watchman held one of the most important positions in the ancient cities of Ezekiel's day. He was to watch over the city and to watch out on the horizon for approaching enemies. When he saw an enemy army approaching, he was to warn the people. The warning was to be immediate, clear, and persistent.

What if a watchman abandoned his post in fear, hiding somewhere in the city? As the enemy destroyed the city and killed its inhabitants, they would ultimately find him. As a reward for his cowardice, the enemy would make the watchman drag into the streets for burning the slain bodies of those he had failed to warn. In the process, his hands, arms, and ultimately his whole body would become soaked with the blood of those for whom he had been responsible. He would often beg for death but even the enemy considered death too good for a coward.

How would you describe Ezekiel's responsibility?

_____

How would you describe your responsibility to the Lord?

_____

Do what you can to tell others the gospel message.

115

To the lost? _____

As you close this study time in prayer, ask God to make you a faithful watchman. In his book *Great Personal Workers* Faris Whitesell tells of the great personal soul-winner, Henry Clay Trumbull. Trumbull is said to have made this his life's resolve:

"I determined that as I loved Christ, and as Christ loved souls, I would press Christ on the individual soul, so that none who were in the proper sphere of my individual responsibility or influence should lack the opportunity of meeting the question whether or not they would individually trust and follow Christ."

What kind of resolve will you make about sharing the gospel?

_____

_____

No one will lack opportunity to answer the question about following Christ.

Day Four
Callous Reactions

"If you do nothing in a difficult time, your strength is limited" (Prov. 24:10).

"Sharing the gospel is just not my thing." How often have you heard, felt, or even made a similar confession yourself? Kingdom Family members realize that sharing the gospel is not an option.

"I'm praying that God will burden me for souls." That's another statement repeated often. But nowhere in the Scripture does God say that sharing the gospel is only for those who are burdened. It is, instead, a simple matter of obedience. Read our focal passage again, this time in light of the compelling realities and critical responsibilities that we have discussed.

Sharing the gospel is never easy. In fact, some of the greatest soul-winners I have ever met have confessed that it was just a difficult in their latter years as it had been in their earlier years. Members of God's Kingdom Family, know that the Adversary always does his best to keep us from doing those things that have Kingdom significance. Is praying easy? Is a consistent quiet time easy?

We find three callous reactions to sharing the gospel that we must avoid. Let's examine each of them.

1. We must not decline to accept our responsibility for sharing the gospel. *"If you do nothing [or give up] in a difficult time, your strength is limited"* (Prov. 24:10).

Have you ever shared the gospel with someone so often that you were just ready to give up? Write about that experience.

_____

_____

Have you ever decided that you just didn't feel like sharing the gospel? ❑ yes   ❑ no

2. We must not delay to accept our responsibility for sharing the gospel. Proverbs 24:11 has a sense of urgency. *Rescue!* God shouts from the pages.

Is delayed obedience still obedience? ❑ yes   ❑ no

Read the following three passages: Numbers 14:21-23; Psalm 95: 7-10; and Hebrews 4:6-7. These passages refer to that moment in Israel's history when they chose to believe in themselves and the ten spies, rather than to believe in God and the two spies.

In His righteous judgment, God sentenced an entire generation (with the exception of the two spies, Joshua and Caleb) to forty years of wandering and, ultimately, death in the wilderness.

The Adversary always tries to keep us from doing Kingdom things.

Was immediate obedience was more important for Israel than it is for you? ❏ yes ❏ no

List some decisions or activities you have been putting off despite God's clear direction.

_____

_____

Now list some people with whom you have been intending to share the gospel but have delayed doing so.

_____

_____

_____

We must not dispute with God about our responsibility of sharing the gospel.

3. We must not dispute with God over our responsibility to share the gospel. *"If you say, 'But we didn't know about this,' won't He who weighs hearts consider it?"* (Prov. 24:12).

How often have you thought of a reasonable excuse for not sharing the gospel? Let me tell you of an experience of my own. I still blush with embarrassment when I think about it.

Once, while serving as a missionary in Africa, I was preparing to speak at a national church retreat. For some reason I didn't sense liberty in my heart. Something was holding me back. As I sought the answer in prayer, God reminded me of a blind man who sat begging each day on a busy street in our town. I always intended to share the gospel with him but it was never the right time. Besides, to share with him I would have to sit right there beside him on that busy street.

Looking back, I am ashamed at the utter wickedness of my heart. I had come seven thousand miles to be a missionary, and now I wouldn't even go a few feet to follow my Master. God just broke my heart in the midst of that dispute, and before the day was over, my sidewalk friend had become my saved brother!

Describe a time in your life when you had a dispute with God.

_____

_____

Who won the dispute? ❑ I did   ❑ God did

Proverbs 24:12 is a reminder that while we are offering our dispute before God, He _____ our hearts.

A calloused heart is one hardened toward the Lord and those He came to save. If you sense that you are calloused toward the Lord or the lost, confess it, and repent.

Day Five
Certain Reckoning

"Won't He who weighs hearts consider it? Won't He who protects your life know?" (Prov. 24:12).

Today is an important day for you. This is the day we bring our study to a close. What's more, we will examine another "day" in the future, the day we each stand before the Judgment Seat of Christ.

Did you know that every believer will one day be judged? This will not be the Great White Throne Judgment, spoken of in Revelation 20:11-15. That judgment is reserved for all unbelievers of all the ages, people whose names are not recorded in the Book of Life. Every person standing in that judgment will spend eternity separated from God.

Read 2 Corinthians 5:10-11. What specific action does Paul say

One day every believer will be judged.

we must take since we will be judged by the Lord who we should honor and fear?

_____

Read 1 Corinthians 3:12.-15. In this passage Paul speaks again of the way we are to work in light of the coming judgment. What does the believer receive if his work survives the "trial by fire?"

What kind

_____

of treasure

Paul speaks in this passage about *gold, silver, precious stones.* Earlier, in Matthew 6:19-20, Jesus spoke about the importance

will you

of laying up *treasure in heaven.*

lay up in

What kind of treasure could you lay up in heaven that would be there to meet you when you arrived?

heaven?

_____

_____

Now, go back to Proverbs 24:12 and consider the judgment we must anticipate. In this verse we discover two things about that time:

1. It is a coming judgment. *"If you say, 'But we didn't know about this,' won't He who weighs hearts consider it?"* As a friend of mine would respond, "That excuse won't fly!"

2. It will be a complete judgment. *"Won't He repay a person according to his work?"* Nothing escapes the Lord's attention.

What emotions fill your heart as you consider the Judgment Seat of Christ?
❑ fear,dread   ❑ anxiety
❑ joyous anticipation ❑ other _____

120

Instead of causing dread in your heart, the fact that such a day is coming and that the judgment will be complete should motivate you to joyful, energetic service. It should encourage you to share the gospel eagerly, leaving the results to the Lord.

Welcome to God's Kingdom Family!
For the past seven weeks you have been coming home to the heart of God, focusing your attention on the very same things that are on His heart, seeking to build your life and home on the Seven Pillars of a Kingdom Family.

Fill in the blanks in the following list of the Seven Pillars of a Kingdom Family.

Honoring _____

Respecting _____

Exercising _____

Serving _____

Using _____

Practicing _____

Sharing _____

Heaven will be a wonderful place! But we have so much more to do as members of God's family and citizens of His kingdom. As Amy Carmichael once wrote from the mission field in India, **"We have all of eternity to celebrate our victories, but only a few minutes before sundown to win them."**

As a member of God's Kingdom Family, by God's grace you can build a Kingdom Family, starting right now, where you are. Welcome home to the heart of God!

Leader Guide

These pages will help you to lead a small group in the study of *Come Home to the Heart of God*. Questions are provided to help get discussion started and to help participants review what they've studied during the week. You will have more questions than time, so choose the questions according to the needs of your small group. Feel free to add your own questions to guide your group.

Introductory Session

- Provide markers and name tags for participants. Make your own name tag now.
- Have workbooks available and place them on the table with the name tags.

1. As people arrive, introduce yourself and direct them to the name tags. Also, have them pick up a workbook, if they don't already have one.
2. After everyone has arrived, welcome the group. Tell them that you are excited about the next seven weeks of study, discussion, and fellowship. Say, "*Come Home to the Heart of God* is an exciting movement to restore the family to God's intended purpose. The end result is a life—and a family—that honors God, lives out His principles, effectively carries the gospel to the nations, and passes along a legacy of faith to succeeding generations.

   "This workbook is based on the Kingdom Family Commitment that we will read in its entirety on page 24 of our workbooks."
3. Read the Kingdom Family Commitment. Read the Preamble and ask several members to read one pillar each until the entire commitment is read.
4. This introductory session will help to lay a foundation for people to share with one another. Ask each person to introduce themselves.
5. The group session will be based on the study from each previous week. Encourage people to do their homework. Say, "You will begin your work tomorrow. On day three, you will be asked to put your Christian testimony in writing. Be prepared to share this in our next session, if you are willing." Be sensitive that you might have group members who are not Christians. They will be led to settle this issue on day two, but at the introductory session, they might show hesitancy.
6. As a leader, set a strong example of being on time, doing your homework, and being willing to share. Be careful to facilitate and not dominate conversation.
7. Tell people they should plan for the group sessions to last about 45 minutes.

Session One
Your Foundation: The Unseen Essential

• Provide markers and name tags. Be sure to wear your name tag as people arrive.

1. Welcome everyone. Begin with prayer, asking God to bless the next six weeks together and especially at session as members share their Christian testimonies.
2. Say, "This week we learned about the foundation of our study and of our faith. I would like us to focus most of our time sharing our Christian testimonies." If someone doesn't volunteer to be first, share your story with the group. Model what others should do by following the format from the workbook.
3. Allow everyone to share who is willing. If you have time, review the seven pillars. This is the foundation for the next six weeks of study. Choose one or two Scriptures from each pillar and have someone read them. Remind the group that they will go into much more detail of each pillar during the next six weeks of study.
4. Have everyone read aloud the Kingdom Family Commitment, found on page 24. After reading it, have participants sign their own books. Participants might ask you to sign their books.
5. Close with prayer, committing yourself and each participant to this study.

Session Two
Honoring God's Authority

• Provide markers and name tags. Be sure to wear your name tag as people arrive.
• If you have a dry-erase board, chalk board, or place to display a poster board, write the name of the first pillar, "Honoring God's Authority."

1. Begin the discussion by reading the first pillar's statement from the Kingdom Family Commitment on page 17.
2. Ask several of the following questions. Try to let as many participants talk as possible. You won't have time to ask every question.
3. We began our look at God's authority by reviewing the story of the Israelites. We often fault them for grumbling and complaining so much. Did you find that you do the same? What are some of the things we grumble about?
4. What does the phrase "other gods besides Me" (Ex. 20:3) mean to you?
5. Have someone read Deuteronomy 6:4-7. Then ask, "How do you impress the commandments on your children?"

6. Who are authority figures in your life? We are told to submit to them. How do we respond to those who definitely are not following God?

7. With day four's lesson, things got personal. How does the issue of disciplining our children relate to God disciplining us?

8. Referring to being in the world but not of it, "This is not a call to have a holier-than-thou attitude, nor is it a call to be weird. It is a call to be different." How can we be different in our world as we seek to share Christ with our unsaved family and friends?

9. Close with prayer, committing each participant to begin to apply what they've learned this week and to be open to what next week's study will provide.

Session Three
Respecting Human Life

- Provide markers and name tags. Be sure to wear your name tag as people arrive.
- If you have a dry-erase board, chalk board, or place to display a poster board, write the name of the second pillar, "Respecting Human Life."

1. Begin the discussion by reading this pillar's statement from the Kingdom Family Commitment on page 18.

2. How did you respond to the story found on page 43?

3. Life is a gift from God. Have someone read Genesis 2:7; Job 33:4; and Psalm 139:13. What do these verses have in common?

4. Ask someone to name the members in their generational "sandwich." How do the members of this family relate to one another? Does each know they are valued? Note: be careful not to put this person on the spot or embarrass him or her in any way.

5. We looked at several verses on day three that reminded us God's presence is always with us. Is that comforting to you? Why or why not?

6. King David charged his son Solomon with several things. What were they? These were found in 1 Kings 2:1-12 in day three.

7. Day four drew us to a familiar story of the prodigal son. Say, "Someone read Luke 15:11-32. Was it a new idea that the father showed genuine interest in both sons? He treated them according to their needs. Which action, found on page 56, would be most difficult for you to do?"

8. The concern for our family members should be modeled after Christ's humility, found in Philippians 2:5-11. Ask someone to read this passage, found on page 59. Discuss how Christ's humble attitude and behavior is an example to us.

9. Close by reading Psalm 139.

Session Four
Exercising Moral Purity

- Provide markers and name tags. Be sure to wear your name tag as people arrive.
- If you have a dry-erase board, chalk board, or place to display a poster board, write the name of the third pillar, "Exercising Moral Purity."

1. Begin the discussion by reading the third pillar's statement from the Kingdom Family Commitment on page 19.
2. Who in this group grew up in a Christian home? What kind of things did you do to learn about Jesus?
3. Ask someone to read 1 Peter 1:15-16. How can we be holy in our world?
4. What are some of the benefits that we have from reading and studying God's Word?
5. What is the difference between *lust* and *love*? Is lust ever good?
6. Regarding the day we looked at marriage, what are the responsibilities of a husband? of a wife?
8. In day five, we learned how important it is to find someone to hold us accountable. The Scripture verse for that day was Proverbs 27:17: *"Iron sharpens iron, and one man sharpens another."* Who sharpens you?
9. Close with prayer, committing each participant to begin to apply what they've learned this week and to be open to what next week's study will provide.

Session Five
Serving My Church

- Provide markers and name tags. Be sure to wear your name tag as people arrive.
- If you have a dry-erase board, chalk board, or place to display a poster board, write the name of the fourth pillar, "Serving My Church."

1. Begin the discussion by reading this pillar's statement from the Kingdom Family Commitment on page 20.
2. What is *church* to you?
3. Although session seven is dedicated solely to learning about sharing the gospel, day three started with the question, "Do you find it easy or difficult to share the gospel?" Ask the group to share their answers.
4. Discuss the phrase *"They had been with Jesus"* (Acts 4:13). Peter and John, ordinary fishermen, were changed dramatically and drastically by following Jesus. What difference do you see in others who you know have "been with Jesus"?

5. Name some of the ways your church has impacted its congregation and community for Christ.
6. Imagine being the recipient of one of Jesus miracles. Before He left, He asked you not to tell anyone about what happened. What would you do?
7. What did Paul challenge the Thessalonians to do in 5:11? How can we do that?
8. Close with prayer, committing each participant to begin to apply what they've learned this week and to be open to what next week's study will provide.

Session Six
Using Time Wisely and Practicing Biblical Stewardship

- Provide markers and name tags. Be sure to wear your name tag as people arrive.
- If you have a dry-erase board, chalk board, or place to display a poster board, write the name of the fifth and sixth pillars, "Using Time Wisely" and "Practicing Biblical Stewardship."

1. Begin the discussion by reading the fifth and sixth pillar's statements from the Kingdom Family Commitment on pages 21-22.
2. What time management help have you tapped into recently? Was it helpful?
3. Ask someone to read Proverbs 3:5-6. Why is it so important to trust the Lord with everything?
4. Day two talked about the importance of seeking the Lord. How do you do that?
5. Whose daily time with the Lord has been influential in your life?
6. What has God placed in your care? Are you being a wise steward over these things?
7. We learned about six areas of responsibility in day four. What are those? Which are the most difficult to do wisely?
8. Were you surprised that it took until day five to hear about stewardship of money? However uncomfortable to hear about, money is part of our stewardship to God. Who has a story like the one shared who learned about tithing?
9. Close with prayer, committing each participant to begin to apply what they've learned this week and to be open to what next week's study will provide.

Session Seven
Sharing the Gospel of Jesus Christ

- Provide markers and name tags. Be sure to wear your name tag as people arrive.
- If you have a dry-erase board, chalk board, or place to display a poster board, write the name of the seventh pillar, "Sharing the Gospel of Jesus Christ."